Colur

Politician, penitent and pilgrim

Anniversary edition
521–2021

Columba

Politician, penitent and pilgrim

521–2021

Ian Bradley

wild goose
publications   www.ionabooks.com

Overseas distribution
Australia: Willow Connection Pty Ltd, Unit 4A, 3–9 Kenneth Road,
Manly Vale, NSW 2093
New Zealand: Pleroma, Higginson Street, Otane 4170,
Central Hawkes Bay

Printed by Bell & Bain, Thornliebank, Glasgow

Contents

Preface

Columba has consistently been Scotland's most popular saint. Immortalised in folklore through Gaelic prayers and poems, he effectively became the emerging nation's patron saint before eventually being trumped by Andrew. His post-Reformation appeal has extended across all Christian denominations, with even the Wee Frees embracing him for his austere, muscular Christianity.

He has held a special fascination for me since childhood, perhaps partly because my mother took me back to her native Argyll to be baptised. I only discovered relatively recently that the church in which this happened, at Toward on the Cowal peninsula, has an unusual, if not unique, stained glass window showing Columba at his moment of death, his right arm being held up by his faithful servant, Diarmit, so that he can give a blessing and his eyes gazing towards heaven from where two angels have descended to meet him. Maybe that powerful image impressed itself on me subliminally as I was held over the font at the age of seventeen months. One of my most abiding childhood memories is of the hand-coloured etching of the saint in his cell on Iona which hung by the front door of our home in Kent and is reproduced on the front cover and at the start of each chapter of this book. The work of Isabel Saul, a Bournemouth-based artist, and exhibited in the Royal Academy in 1926, it depicts Columba, his bald head surrounded by a shining halo, sitting at his desk in his monk's habit copying out a psalm. At his feet are the crane whose flight to the island he prophesied to the monks and a sprig of oak possibly intended to symbolise his pre-Christian druidic inheritance, while in the background is the faithful white horse which came up to him and shed tears on the last day of his life. My father saw it in a London shop window and bought it as a present for my mother shortly before their wedding at St Columba's Church in London on 11 June 1949. I myself was married in the same church thirty-six years later on 20 July 1985.

It is a very idealised portrait, almost icon-like, exuding a sense of calm, peace and sanctity and it lends itself to quiet contemplation and meditation. Yet one of the things that has long attracted me to Columba is that he is not just a plaster saint but a very human character with evident faults and flaws. According to the Irish folklorist Dáithí Ó hÓgáin, in Irish tradition he was popularly regarded 'as having been a short-tempered saint'.[1] He is certainly portrayed by his biographers as having an irascible side. As we shall see, like most of us, his character was full of complexity, ambiguities and contradictions. This to me makes him more interesting, more real and more relevant than many saints of the church.

The first edition of this book appeared in 1997, having been commissioned by the Iona Community to mark the 1400th anniversary of Columba's death on Iona on 9 June 597. This substantially revised and updated version is being published in 2021 to commemorate the 1500th anniversary of his birth. There is, in fact, considerable uncertainty about exactly when he was born. If you put the question to Google, it comes up with the precise date of 7 December 521 in large bold type as though there were no doubt about it. Manus O'Donnell in his Irish life of the saint published in 1532 was the first to propose this date and although it has been widely taken up, there are those who believe that Columba may have been born a year or two earlier.

There is also some uncertainty as to exactly where he was born. Again, O'Donnell is very precise that it was at Rath Cnó near Gartan in the land of the Cenél Conaill, the prominent family of which Columba was a leading member. Gartan, which lies in a remote area of lakes and hills in the north of Donegal close to what is now the Glenveagh National Park in the north west corner of Ireland, was first identified as Columba's birthplace in the twelfth-century Irish life of the saint. The actual spot where his mother Eithne gave birth to him is supposedly marked by a large cup-marked flagstone which stands in a field on a hillside above Lough Gartan known as Lacknacoo. According to Manus O'Donnell, 'the flagstone was under him at his birth. The baby lay cross-wise on it and the flag opened so as to make a space for him, and the figure of a cross is on the flagstone from that time to this. This flagstone has remained in that place working miracles and wonders.'[2] According to local tradition, in the nineteenth century those about to emigrate would spend their last night in Ireland sleeping on the stone, which became known as *Leac na Cumhadh* (the Stone of Sorrows), out of a sense of solidarity with Columba the exile and a conviction that he would make their own sorrow at leaving their mother country easier to bear.

A large Celtic cross, erected in 1912 close to the *Leac na Cumhadh*, marks the supposed birthplace which can be accessed via signposted minor roads. A mile or so away on the southern shore of Lough Gartan the Colmcille Heritage Centre provides a good introduction to the stories and legends about Columba's early life. We know much less about the four decades that he spent in Ireland than about his last thirty or so years on Iona. This means that there is more room for invention, speculation and romantic imagination. It also means that this book concentrates very much on the latter half of the saint's life which is so well documented by his biographer, or more accurately hagiographer, Adomnán, and by others associated with the early Iona monastic community.

It is appropriate that this book has been commissioned and published by the modern-day Iona Community which is living out Columba's active and contemplative Christianity today. I have derived much spiritual succour over the last three or more decades from the witness and worship of the Community, of which I am an associate member. I am grateful to Sandra Kramer, publishing manager of Wild Goose Publications, for her enthusiastic support for this new edition and to the Wild Goose Resource Group for allowing me to reprint the hymn 'From Erin's shores Columba came'. I am also particularly grateful to Thomas Owen Clancy and Gilbert Márkus for their kindness in allowing me to quote from their translations of early Latin and Irish poems from Iona.

1 *Spes Scotorum: Hope of Scots. Saint Columba, Iona and Scotland* edited by Dauvit Brown and Thomas Owen Clancy (T & T Clark, Edinburgh, 1999), p.256

2 Manus O'Donnell, *Betha Coluim Chille*, edited and translated by G.Schoepperle (University of Illinois, Urbana, 1918), p.52

A brief chronology of Columba's life

(All dates are approximate)

521   Born in Gartan, Donegal

561   Battle of Cúl Drebene between Northern and Southern Uí Néill

563   Leaves Ireland and comes to Scotland

574   Ordains Aédhán mac Gabhráin king of Scots Dál Riata

575   Attends convention of Druim Ceat

587   Founds monastery at Durrow

597   Death on Iona

The main sources for Columba's life and work

(*In roughly chronological order*)

Amra Choluimb Chille (The Elegy of Colum Cille) – probably written around 600 by Dallán Forgaill, an Irish poet.

Fo Réir Choluimb and *Tiugraind Beccáin* – two poems probably written around 650 by Beccán mac Luigdech, a hermit associated with the Iona community and possibly living on Rum.

The Irish Annals (especially those of Ulster and Tigernach) – chronicle events in Ireland and were probably begun around the middle of the seventh century, although some historians believe that a chronicle written on Iona and possibly started during Columba's lifetime may underlie the earliest stratum of the *Irish Annals* up to c.740.

Book of the Miracles of Columba – probably written in the 630s or 640s by Cumméne, seventh abbot of Iona, who died in 679. Only a tiny fragment of this survives. It was almost certainly an important source for Adomnán.

Vita Columbae – the classic life written by Adomnán, eighth abbot of Iona, between 688 and 692.

Ecclesiastical History of the English People – written by the Venerable Bede in Jarrow and completed in 731.

The Irish Life of Columba – a sermon in Irish based on Genesis 12.1 and possibly written in Derry in the eleventh or twelfth centuries, although some historians date it as early as the ninth century. The oldest surviving text is in a fifteenth-century manuscript, *Leabhar Breac* (Speckled Book), housed in the Royal Irish Academy.

Betha Coluim Chille – a life of Columba compiled in Ireland in 1532 by Manus O'Donnell, a leading figure in the O'Donnell clan, descendants of the Cenél Conaill of whom Columba was a member. It incorporated material from a number of earlier Irish sources.

One

Columba's journey –
pilgrimage, penitence or politics?

In or around the year 563 AD a middle-aged and rather well-connected monk set off with a few companions in a small boat from the shores of his native Donegal, in the north west tip of Ireland, to brave the Atlantic swell. It is not clear where he was heading for, nor how long it was before he reached his ultimate destination, the tiny island of Iona off the west coast of Scotland, about 100 miles away from his starting point. This journey is rightly perceived as one of the most significant events in the early history, and more particularly the early Christian history, of the British Isles. The monastery which Columba founded on Iona was to become one of the great spiritual powerhouses of early medieval Christendom, a beacon of Christian enlightenment and culture which shone brightly through the period which was long described by historians as the Dark Ages. Iona became the base for the evangelisation of not just much of modern Scotland but also, through its daughter foundation at Lindisfarne off the north Northumbrian coast, of large parts of northern and central England. Together with the other monasteries which Columba founded, it was also to play a key role in secular as well as ecclesiastical affairs, supporting the royal house which eventually provided the first rulers of the united kingdom of Scotland. Columba himself was to become a cult figure, venerated throughout Scotland and Ireland for his miraculous works, his sanctity and his protective powers.

Columba's reason for leaving the comparative comfort and security of Ireland in his early forties to start a new life in a wilder and less hospitable region is unclear and has been the subject of much speculation and controversy. Modern psychologists might well see it in terms of a classic midlife crisis in which someone approaching middle age and bored with their conventional existence seeks a new challenge. Yet there is nothing to suggest that Columba had become fed up with life in Ireland where he seems to have been deeply involved in monastic life and also to have taken an active interest in political affairs. Others might point to the sense of 'wanderlust' in the Celtic temperament which has led so many Irish and Scots to leave their native shores. Having reached Iona, however, he seems to have settled there and not to have done any more travelling, apart from occasional visits back to Ireland and into the Scottish Highlands and Islands on political and ecclesiastical business. He did not have the restless spirit of other notable Irish saints, like his contemporaries Brendan of Clonfert, who journeyed far across the Atlantic, and Columbanus, who set off from his monastery in Bangor around 590 for a lengthy progress across Europe.

Columba's departure from Ireland seems to have marked a turning point in his life and at least one historian has used the language of conversion to explain this change of direction. Alfred Smyth writes of this episode: 'We seem to be dealing with a classic conversion story, involving not necessarily the conversion of a great sinner to repentance, but the giving at least of a new intensity to a life already dedicated to the church. For Columba, like Paul, or even like Christ or Mohammed, seems to have waited to translate his fervent sense of mission into action when he reached middle age, and from then on his life took a radically new direction.'[1] Yet there is no evidence that he did, in fact, undergo any kind of dramatic religious experience prior to his departure from Ireland. Unlike Patrick, who according to his own *Confession* was called in a vision to evangelise the Irish, Columba is not portrayed by any of his biographers as having received a direct call from God to cross the sea to Pictland and evangelise its heathen inhabitants. Indeed, as we shall see, there is some doubt as to whether he saw himself principally as a missionary. Nor did the nature of his life change quite as much after 563 as some commentators have suggested. On Iona, he seems to have gone on doing the same kind of things that he had been involved in during his years in Ireland – praying, copying manuscripts, offering pastoral care and spiritual leadership, founding and running monastic communities and playing a high-profile role in the dynastic disputes and political rivalries of Irish and British kings and chieftains.

Perhaps it is to Columba's near contemporaries that we should turn for an explanation as to what motivated his fateful journey that ended on Iona. Their writings about him have a very different perspective from those of modern commentators and emphasise two of the most important themes in what has, for better or worse, come to be known as Celtic Christianity – pilgrimage and penitence. Both of these themes derive from the essentially monastic culture of early Irish Christianity and its stress on asceticism and holiness, self-discipline and sacrifice. The early sources convey a sense that Columba made his journey from Ireland to Iona as a pilgrim and a penitent. They suggest that there was both a voluntary and perhaps also an enforced element in his exile from his beloved native land and that in leaving Ireland he may have been atoning for some misdemeanour, as well as renouncing the comfort and security of home.

The briefest and most factual account of the journey comes from the pen of Adomnán, abbot of Iona from 679 to 704, and portrays Columba as a voluntary exile and a pilgrim: 'In the second year after the battle of Cúl Drebene (fought AD 561), and in the forty-second year of his age, St Columba, resolving to seek a foreign country for the love of Christ, sailed from Ireland to Britain.'[2] The concept of *peregrinatio* (the Latin word which Columba and his contemporaries used) was very different from pilgrimage as we think of it today. It was not a matter of going off to perceived holy places to experience a spiritual buzz or 'high'. For the early Irish monks pilgrimage was rather a perpetual exile from the comforts and distractions of the world. It was, indeed, a way of bearing witness to Christ and a kind of martyrdom in which Christians separated themselves from all that they loved for the sake of God. Pilgrimage had clear penitential overtones: it was often undertaken at the instigation of a soul-friend or confessor with the object of purging the individual *peregrinus* of worldly attachments and affections.

Pilgrimage of this kind had a particular appeal to Columba's fellow countrymen. In the words of the historian Thomas Charles-Edwards, *'peregrinatio* was the most intelligible form of ascetic renunciation available to Irishmen'.[3] This was because of the strength of family ties and landed wealth, the importance of local patriotism and the legal bars to travel which were such marked features of early medieval Irish society. There was also a clear scriptural basis behind their desire for exile and pilgrimage. In the Gospels Jesus repeatedly calls on those who would follow him to leave home and family. Perhaps an even more direct influence on the Irish *peregrini* was the Old Testament narrative of the journey of the people of Israel through the wilderness and across the desert. God's words to Abraham, 'Leave your own country, your kin, and your father's house' (Genesis 12.1) were often quoted in connection with the journeys undertaken by Irish monks. Indeed, they provided the inspiration for the mid-twelfth-century *Irish Life* of Columba which took the form of an extended meditation on this particular text. It was not, however, towards a land flowing with milk and honey that many Irish *peregrini* felt led. Rather they sought out desolate, isolated, barren places where they stayed for a while in caves or cells before moving on again. Another influence was important here – the example of the Egyptian desert fathers like St Antony who had established a pattern of discipleship based on withdrawal from the world and solitary contemplation.[4]

Columba's journey in 563 does not seem to have involved quite such a radical act of discipleship as was made by the desert fathers.

He did not opt for the solitary life himself, although he may well have spent periods living alone in cells around the west coast of Scotland both before and after moving to Iona and he certainly encouraged the practice of the eremitical (hermit-like) solitary life in his monastic foundations. Yet if he did not cut himself off from human companionship and worldly concerns, his journey from Ireland does seem to have involved an element of exile, whether voluntary or imposed.

Several of the poems written about Columba in the century or so after his death portray his journey from Ireland as both an epic adventure and an act of purgation and self-denial. These two elements are particularly marked in the poems attributed to Beccán mac Luigdech, a hermit associated with the Iona community who possibly resided on the island of Rum in the mid-seventh century. One of them dramatically evokes the power of the Atlantic swell into which Columba and his companions launched themselves:

> In scores of curraghs with an army of wretches
> he crossed the long-haired sea.
> He crossed the wave-strewn wild region,
> foam-flecked, seal-filled,
> Savage, bounding, seething, white-tipped, pleasing,
> doleful.[5]

Another of the poems attributed to Beccán, *Fo Réir Choluimb* (Bound to Columba), pursues this imagery of the ocean's wildness to suggest that Columba was purging himself:

> He crucified – not for crimes –
> his body on the grey waves ...
> He left Ireland, made a pact,

he crossed in ships the whale's shrine.
He shattered lusts – it shone on him –
a bold man over the sea's ridge.[6]

Beccán, it will be noted, goes out of his way to emphasise that Columba's self-sacrificial journey was not made in any way to atone for crimes. Several historians, however, have drawn a rather different conclusion on the basis of remarks made in Adomnán's *Life* and in the *Annals of Ulster*. They have suggested that Columba's departure from Ireland may have been forced on him as a way of either atoning for or escaping from the consequences of some crime or misdemeanour in which he had been complicit because of his involvement in family feuds and dynastic disputes. This is by no means inconceivable. We know that he had an aristocratic background. His father, Fedelmid, was a prominent member of the powerful and bellicose Uí Néill clan who effectively ruled Donegal and was said to have been the great-grandson of the semi-legendary Neill of the Nine Hostages, high king of Ireland in the fifth century. Columba's mother, Eithne, also came from a prominent noble family. He grew up very conscious of this heritage and it is quite possible that over-enthusiastic clan and family loyalty got him into trouble.

Of key importance to this interpretation of why he had to leave Ireland is the battle of Cúl Drebene mentioned by Adomnán as having taken place two years before Columba's departure. This battle, which took place near Sligo, was one of the most important skirmishes in a long and bloody struggle between two powerful dynasties for control of Ireland. It reminds us that Columba's era was an age of warlords as well as saints. Ireland at this time was made up of around 150 *túaths* or small kingships, each with fierce tribal and clan loyalty to their ruler. Over them was the *rí Temro*, or high king of Ireland. This position was claimed by the Uí Néill, the family from which Columba himself came, but it was disputed between their northern and southern branches.

In the battle of Cúl Drebene in 561 the ruler of the Southern Uí Néill, Diarmait mac Cerbaill, sometimes described as the last of the Irish high kings to reign from the pagan sanctuary of Tara, was decisively defeated by a coalition led by the king of Connaught and leading members of the northern Uí Néill, among whom were Columba's first cousin and his uncle. According to the *Annals of Tigernach* the victors 'prevailed through the prayers of Columba' which miraculously drove away a mist conjured by pagan priests to conceal Diarmait's advancing army. Several historians have suggested that it was not just prayers that Columba offered to his kinsmen and that he may also have taken part in the fighting. There are several pieces of evidence for this. According to Adomnán, Columba had a 'livid scar, which remained on his side all the days of his life'. Was this the result of a wound sustained at Cúl Drebene or at some other fracas between the northern Uí Néill and their southern rivals? Adomnán also writes of Columba being excommunicated from the church for certain 'trivial and pardonable' offences and being made to appear at a synod held at Teltown in County Meath. Those convening the synod apparently dropped the charges against him after evidence was brought of supernatural signs of his favour in the eyes of God. Adomnán seems to have concluded the chapter in which he described this event with the statement: 'About that same time the holy man, with his twelve disciples and fellow soldiers, sailed across to Britain.'[7]

It is tempting to draw the conclusion from this evidence that Columba's departure from Ireland was bound up with his censure by the Synod of Teltown and may well have been imposed on him as a penance and a condition for his return to full communion with the church. But what was the offence for which he was excommunicated and for which he may have been forced to leave his native shores? Was it his involvement in the battle of Cúl Drebene or was it rather, as Adomnán implies, something more 'trivial and pardonable'? A possible answer to this question, which exonerates Columba from direct involvement in the battle but links to the dynastic rivalry between the northern and southern Uí Néills, lies in the oft-repeated story of the illegally copied psalter.

This story recounts that the offence for which Columba found himself hauled before the Synod of Teltown involved the unauthorised copying of a beautiful book of psalms which St Finnian had brought back from Rome and placed in the church of his monastery at Moville in County Down. Columba is said to have stolen into the church late at night sometime in the year 560 and in certain versions of the story he is accused of having taken away the psalter and failing to return it. Finnian apparently appealed to his protector and high king, Diarmait mac Cerbaill of the Southern Uí Néill, who censured Columba and demanded the book's return and the surrender of the copy that he had made. Columba refused at least this second request and was backed by his northern Uí Néill cousins who were spoiling for a fight with their arch-rival Diarmait. In some accounts this incident is portrayed as sparking off the battle of Cúl Drebene. The story is not totally beyond the bounds of credulity. We know how deeply attached Columba was to the Book of Psalms and how much of his time was spent copying psalters. There is a tradition that he underwent part of his monastic training at Finnian's monastery in Moville, which had been founded in 540, and it is not inconceivable that he could have been back there as a fully professed monk. It seems curious and uncharacteristic, however, that he did not seek permission before copying the psalter. What may be more significant is the link made between Columba and the bloodshed at Cúl Drebene. Whether the incident involving the psalter is true or not, the impression given by the various versions of this story is that the saint carried a certain responsibility for the battle between the northern and southern Uí Néills and had blood on his hands. Later sources suggest that Columba felt a deep sense of remorse and willingly accepted the penance of lifelong exile from Ireland as an atonement for his sins.

The question of Columba's involvement in the battle of Cúl Drebene is a matter of debate among historians and it is important to point out that several regard it as a complete red herring in terms of the reasons for his journey. However, whether there was anything to it or not, it highlights the importance of his royal blood and aristocratic connections. If he had not opted for the monastic life, or had it chosen for him by his parents, Columba would almost certainly have been ruler of a *túath* and might well have been high king of Ireland. His particular branch of the Uí Néill family, the Cenél Conaill, rose to prominence in 566, five years after the battle of Cúl Drebene and three years after his departure from Ireland, when his first cousin, Ainmere mac Sétnai, became high king. The dynasty of Cenél Conaill survived as one of the main royal houses of Ireland until the seventeenth century.

In one of the most detailed academic studies of this period, Máire Herbert has suggested that it was Columba's royal connections that prompted his journey from Ireland to Iona in a spirit of pilgrimage. Dismissing the notion that his departure was linked either with the battle of Cúl Drebene or the Teltown Synod, she writes: 'One may suppose that the Uí Néill churchman perceived that his family connections made it difficult for him to remain apart from the public arena, and to pursue the ideals of monasticism. Therefore, as renunciation of wealth and claims to kingship in Ireland no longer seemed to suffice as ascetic ideals, he sought a *potioris peregrinationis locus* overseas.'[8]

Columba's royal connections could point to quite another

reason for his journey to Iona. He may have gone to help consolidate the new Irish kingdom being established across the sea and to forge close links between its rulers and the northern Uí Néill. In making the relatively short sea crossing from Ulster to the west coast of Scotland, he was following in the wake of a substantial number of his countrymen. These Irish migrants (known by their Roman name of *Scoti*) came particularly from the *túath* or kingdom of Dál Riata in Antrim. By the time of Columba's birth enough of them had settled in their new home to form the nucleus of a second kingdom of Dál Riata whose boundaries corresponded with the modern region of Argyll. As abbot of Iona, Columba was to be instrumental in building up the power of the rulers of this new Scottish kingdom and in forging a close alliance between them and his own northern Uí Néill kinsmen in Ulster. It is quite possible that he went there initially for largely political reasons, either at the behest of the king of Scots Dál Riata, Conall mac Comgaill, or of his own royal relatives. As his most recent biographer, Tim Clarkson, writes: 'Columba found it hard to disentangle his religious vocation from his loyalty to his powerful kinsmen in Donegal. He might therefore have been perceived by Conall not so much as a holy pilgrim as an ambassador representing his family's political inerests.'[9]

Historians are now generally agreed that Columba did not make directly for Iona when he left Ireland in 563. There is a romantic story that he left his beloved homeland as a penitential pilgrim determined never to look on it again and sailed from island to island until reaching Iona, the first from which there was no view back, giving the hill above the bay where he landed the name Càrn Cúil ri Eirinn (the hill with its back to Ireland), but this only surfaced in the late eighteenth century. It is much more likely that he headed first for the mainland of Argyll and only later went to Iona. There is a reference in the *Annals of Ulster*, which were quite possibly composed on Iona, to Conall mac Comgaill, king of Dál Riata from 558 to 574, granting the island of Iona to Columba in 574. It is significant that the first incident Adomnán records after describing Columba leaving Ireland is a meeting between the saint and this king. This would almost certainly have taken place at one of Dál Riata's royal palaces or forts on the Argyll mainland. Alfred Smyth goes so far as to suggest that Columba did not move to Iona until the beginning of the reign of Conall's successor, Aédán mac Gabráin, in 574, eleven years after he had left Ireland.[10]

The shortest and least hazardous sea crossing between Ireland and Scotland is from the north east coast of Antrim to the southern tip of the Mull of Kintyre, a distance of just twelve miles. The notion that this was the route taken by Columba in 563 is supported by the existence of a ruined chapel and a well, both bearing Columba's name, close to the shore at Keil Point on the southern tip of Kintyre near the village of Southend. Nearby are two footprints carved on a rocky outcrop. Known as St Columba's footprints, they supposedly mark the place where he first set foot in Scotland, having sailed into either Dunaverty or Caskay Bay. The more southerly footprint is laid parallel to the shore with the other, now largely eroded, at a 90 degree angle to it and the date 564 carved between them. In fact, while the first footprint probably dates back to the first millennium BC, the other more northerly one was apparently carved by a local stonemason in 1885. He may also have added the date although there are suggestions that it was carved in the sixteenth century. Beside the footprints are what look like the outline or foundations of a small rectangular building. Could this conceivably have been a cell or chapel built by Columba when he landed here? This is unlikely – anything dating from his time would not usually have been built with stone. The footprints, along with the adjoining chapel and well, were probably attributed and dedicated to Columba several hundred years after his death, either in the twelfth century or later in the Middle Ages, when the parish of Kilcomkill was established, perhaps by the MacDonald lords of the Isles.

Yet even if Columba did not create either of these footprints himself, it is quite possible that he stood in the older one looking up towards the fortress of Dunaverty, a stronghold of the Dál Riatan kings perched on top of the rocky cliffs which loom over Keil Point. Tim Clarkson speculates that the older footprint may have been used at royal inaugurations with the nearby well providing water for sacred anointings, first by pagan priests and later by their Christian successors. He suggests that it may have been here that Aédán's anointing as king took place, an event which Adomnán described Columba presiding over on Iona. He also posits Dunaverty as Aédán's capital in Kintyre and the *caput regionis* where, according to Adomnán, Columba met sailors from Gaul.[11]

Other historians believe that the *caput regionis* was Dunadd in the Kilmartin valley near the modern town of Lochgilphead. A hill fort and centre of royal power with two carved footprints on its summit, this could also have been where Columba met King Conall soon after arriving from Ireland. Given his close links with Dál Riatan royalty, it seems highly probable that Columba would have visited Dunadd. An early settlement known as Kilmahumaig, less than three miles from Dunadd and at one time annexed to Kilmartin parish, seems to have been dedicated to Columba and provides further possible evidence of his association with this area. So too does the proximity of one of the most romantic and evocative places which bears his name, St Columba's cave on the shore of Loch Caolisport near Ellary in Knapdale. There are in fact two caves on this site. In his book *Celtic Scotland*, William Skene suggested that Columba might have used one as a chapel and the other as a dwelling place when visiting King Conall at Dunadd which is just nine miles away. The Argyll historian Mary Donaldson believed that Conall might, in fact, have had his fortress on top of An Torr at the head of Loch Caolisport and less than two miles from the caves.[12]

There has been speculation that the bay in front of the caves rather than the Mull of Kintyre may have been where Columba first landed in Argyll. Excavations suggest that the caves were occupied as early as 5500 BC. A considerable quantity of pottery from the early iron age points to more intensive use and occupation between c.500 BC and 400 AD. The caves seem next to have been used in the seventh and eighth centuries by Christians, possibly hermits or itinerant preachers with Columban affiliations. They were probably responsible for carving the crosses which can still be seen on the rock face at the back of the main cave and turning it into a chapel by erecting an altar on a rock shelf. Several authors have attributed the carvings to Columba himself but archaeologists are disinclined to date them so early. From the ninth century Norsemen apparently stored their boats in the caves and probably slept in them – a rare Viking balance has been found in the larger one. In the twelfth century Christians seem to have returned to them and in the following century a chapel was built by the entrance to the main cave, the ruins of which are still visible. Much later the caves were used by fishermen to store their nets. They are now a place of pilgrimage, with occasional services being held there by Roman Catholics, Episcopalians and Presbyterians.

Some historians think that before moving to Iona Columba spent time on the unidentified island of Hinba. It was certainly a place with which he seems to have had a close and consistent connection. Adomnán describes him founding a monastery there, to which he later sent his uncle Ernan as abbot, and making frequent visits, both to escape from the hustle and bustle of Iona by going on solitary retreat and also to meet other important Christian leaders. It was on Hinba that he celebrated the Eucharist with four prominent monastic founders, Brendan, Cormac, Cainnech and Comgall, who had come from Ireland to visit him. Hinba was also where Columba experienced over a space of three days and nights an intense concentration of angelic visions which revealed many secrets and made plain passages from Scripture. Hinba clearly played an important part in Columba's life. On the basis of his reading of Adomnán, Alfred Smyth proposed that it was Columba's first base in Scotland and that he did not move from there to Iona until the beginning of Aédán's reign in 574. John Marsden in his book *Sea Roads of the Saints* also puts the foundation of Hinba before that of Iona. Among the islands which have been proposed as the location of Hinba are Gunna, which lies between Coll and Tiree; Eileach an Naoimh in the Garvellach islands in the Firth of Lorn, where an isolated early grave is said to be that of Columba's mother, Eithne; Eilean Shona in Loch Moidart; Canna, where there is a medieval church dedicated to Columba at A'Chill, the main settlement on the island; and Seil on the east side of the Firth of Lorn and now linked to the mainland by a bridge. Most historians, however, tend to favour either Colonsay/Oronsay or Jura. Both Alan Macquarrie, who devotes an interesting chapter to the question in his book *The Saints of Scotland*, and Richard Sharpe, editor of the most recent edition of Adomnán's *Life*, opt for Oronsay/Colonsay.

I myself am strongly inclined to agree with William Watson and other Celtic scholars that Hinba is, in fact, Jura. There are several pieces of evidence supporting this theory. Adomnán states that Ernan, Columba's uncle, was abbot there. The main graveyard on Jura, on the site of what is thought to have been the earliest ecclesiastical settlement on the island, which lies above the main settlement at Craighouse and near the old crofting township of Keils, is called Kilearnadil. Local tradition has it that Ernan wished to be buried on the island and that his body was transported back from Iona where he had died on a visit, landed on a rock known as Leac Earnan at the south end of Jura and carried to Kilearnadil. Both the well and the ecclesiastical settlement at Tarbert, half way up Jura, seem to have been dedicated to Columba from an early period. Lowlandmen's Bay, situated between Craighouse and Tarbert on the island's east coast, perfectly fits Adomnán's description of the Muirbolc Már, or 'great bag-like bay', on Hinba. Watson further argues that Hinba was named after the Old Irish word *inbe* meaning an incision and that this must have been suggested by some distinctive topographical feature. Jura is virtually bisected by Loch Tarbert which presents a more dramatic example of such an incision than is found on any other island off Argyll.

One possible reason for there being a delay between Columba leaving Ireland and settling on Iona could be that in 563 the island was still in the hands of the native (and pagan) Picts. The Anglo-Saxon historian Bede states twice in his *Ecclesiastical History of the English Speaking People* that it was, in fact, the Picts who gave Iona to Columba. However, this is generally regarded as unlikely. It may be that the island was still under Pictish control when Columba arrived from Ireland and it seems most likely that it was the king of Dál Riata, Conall mac Comgaill, who gave it to him as a site for his new monastery, even if Irish rule over the island had to be established before he could take up residence there.

As well as there being some uncertainty as to when Columba went to Iona, it is also unclear what the island was like when he did settle there and establish his monastery. Bede states that it contained 'about five families' although Adomnán and some other later sources suggest that it was uninhabited, which seems unlikely. According to the medieval *Irish Life* of Columba there were Druids living on the island. In 1693 John Fraser, Dean of the Isles, suggested that Columba had deliberately built his monastery on the site of an existing Druid school or college and even taken over this pre-Christian institution. The notion that there were already Druids on Iona, suggested by the early name of the area near Martyrs' Bay, Cladh nan Drunnich, or the Druids' Burial Place, appealed strongly to eighteenth-century syncretists and romantics who pointed out that the ancient Greek historian Plutarch had written around 100 AD about an island of holy men close to the coast. Radio-carbon dating undertaken in 1988 suggests that there was an enclosure dating from the first or second century AD covering roughly the same area as that bounded by the later monastic ditch or *vallum*.

The extent to which Columba and his contemporaries consciously took over some of the roles and institutions of pre-Christian Druids and bards and worked with and adapted some of their belief systems rather than repudiating them is hotly debated by scholars. It is part of a much wider debate as to whether Celtic Christianity represented continuity with or radical rejection of pre-Christian Celtic religion. Columba has often been portrayed as uniting the Celtic traditions of the *Fianna*, heroic warriors, and the *Filidhean*, poets with a priestly calling. Some modern writers have followed Charles Plummer and other earlier Celtic scholars in portraying him essentially as a Christianised Druid, gifted with second sight. In this reading, the angels with whom he communed take over the role of the fairies of pre-Christian Celtic mythology. But others see him as having had no truck at all with pagan beliefs and practices and as confronting rather than adapting them. In their view, if he did, indeed, build his monastery on the site of a Druid school or college, it was deliberately to obliterate the old religion and replace it with the new.

I have dwelt at some length on the confusing and ultimately unresolved questions of why Columba left Ireland and how and when he came to Iona for two specific reasons quite apart from their intrinsic interest. Firstly, they alert us to the great difficulty of disentangling fact from legend and show the degree to which the sources for his life are scanty and confusing. Secondly, they introduce the dominant features that made up his complex character – part pilgrim, part penitent and part politician. The saint of Iona remained very much the diplomat and power-broker, dabbling in dynastic politics and sometimes acting like a proud warlord while at the same time spending hours in prayer, meticulously copying psalms, grinding corn and washing the feet of his monks.

If this suggests a split personality, then it is certainly true that Columba's character, in so far as we can discern it through the layers of legend and veneration that have built up over the centuries, displays a number of contradictions. He never lost the attributes of the warrior aristocracy into which he had been born and retained to the end of his life an autocratic imperiousness, a hasty temper, a fierce pride and a lingering attachment to the 'fascinating rattle of a complicated battle'. Yet he could also be gentle, humble and overflowing with Christian charity. This juxtaposition is perhaps the basis for the tradition which appears in some later sources that he had two Gaelic names: first *Crimthann* (the fox) and later *Columcille* (the dove of the church). It is just conceivable that the earlier name may reflect pagan origins and that he acquired the second on being baptised as a Christian but this must be conjecture. The characteristics of both the fox and the dove continued to manifest themselves throughout his life. They are well captured in a hymn to commemorate him written more than seventy years ago by John Hannah, a priest in the Scottish Episcopal Church. I have often sung it with groups to bring to life Columba's complex and seemingly ambiguous personality – I suggest singing the first verse to the strong martial tune 'Austrian Hymn' and the second to the gentler 'Abbot's Leigh' to bring out the contrast even more.

Who is this so fierce and warlike,
Slow to mercy, swift to chide?
See him rouse the clans to battle
To avenge his wounded pride.
'Tis the crafty warrior, Crimthann,
Spreading hatred far and wide.
Evil passions seek to brand him,
And his maker's image hide.

Who is this so strong and gentle,
Rich in prayer and wise in lore?
See, the very beasts befriend him
As he walks Iona's shore!
'Tis Columba, saint and abbot,
With the Cross the Saviour bore;
He proclaims throughout our homeland
Holy Gospel's wondrous store.[13]

If we are to encounter the true Columba, we need to acknowledge this ambiguity and to come face to face with *Crimthann* as well as *Columcille*. He was no plaster saint but an intensely human figure with faults and weaknesses as well as extraordinary depths of gentleness and humility. For his biographer Ian Finlay, 'there is nothing inconsistent in believing Columba was both a truly great Christian evangelist and teacher and also an ambitious and resolute statesman. Nor is there any reason why he should not have been tender, devoted, angelic, and yet passionate, irascible and, on occasion, even ruthless in achieving his ends. The Celtic temperament runs to extremes.'[14]

Alongside the excesses of the Celtic psyche, we can perhaps point to another feature of the outlook of the early Irish monks to help explain one aspect of what might seem a double life. They understood the basic rhythm of Christian life and the need to balance activity in the world with withdrawal from it. The ideal of *peregrinatio* involved a certain degree of exile, renunciation and searching for one's own desert place of resurrection. Except for those few called permanently to the solitary eremitical life of the anchorite, however, it did not mean a complete withdrawal from the world and its affairs. The monastic life was far from being one of retreat and escape. Indeed, monasteries were almost certainly the busiest institutions in Celtic society, constantly teeming with people and fulfilling the roles of school, library, hospital, guest house, arts centre and mission station. Most of the great Celtic saints alternated between periods of intense activity and involvement in administrative affairs and lengthy spells of quiet reflection and months spent alone in a cell on a remote island or rocky promontory. In this, they were following the example of their Lord and Saviour, one moment surrounded by crowds and engaged in preaching, teaching and healing, and the next walking alone by the lakeside or engaged in quiet prayer in the hills.

Columba's life exemplified this balance and rhythm. At times he was busily engaged in founding monasteries, negotiating with kings, attending councils, going on missionary journeys and ruling his ever-expanding monastic *familia*. Yet his biographers also portray him spending long periods praying or copying the Scriptures in his cell and frequently taking himself to Hinba for solitary retreats. In many ways this combination of action and meditation provided a perfect example of what modern theologians call 'praxis' – a combination of involvement in practical issues and theological reflection. In the words of a poem written about him just a year or two after his death, 'What he conceived keeping vigil, by action he ascertained.'[15]

To a considerable extent these two sides of Columba's character were the product of his noble birth and monastic training. He mixed as easily with warlords and princes as with monks and scholars. Through his veins coursed the blood of a long line of fierce pagan warriors. It would hardly be surprising if this element in his make-up sometimes came to the surface and caused him to do things which he may later have regretted. His upbringing, however, was very largely if not entirely monastic. He seems to have spent his boyhood and teenage years being tutored by priests and living in monastic foundations. This in itself was not particularly unusual. The children of the Irish warrior aristocracy were generally fostered out to tutors for their education. Sixty years or so before Columba's birth Patrick noted in his *Confession* that 'sons and daughters of Scottic [i.e. Irish] chieftains are seen to become monks and virgins for Christ'.[16] Columba probably belonged to the sixth or seventh generation which had known Christianity in Ireland. By 431 the Christian community on the island was large enough for the pope to send out a bishop called Palladius to oversee it. Some years later Patrick began his work of evangelisation which seems to have spread across much of the country. He is generally credited with giving the church in Ireland an organised diocesan structure, although within a generation of his death in or around 493 this seems to have broken down and the dominant institution in Irish Christianity had become the monastery.

The middle years of the sixth century saw the founding of several of the great monastic houses in Ireland which were to dominate the Christian landscape of the island for the next five hundred years. Among them were Moville, set up by Finnian in 540, and Clonmacnoise, established by Ciarán in 548. This was the world in which Columba grew up and received his training. We know tantalisingly little about his early life. Adomnán reports that as a boy he was effectively brought up by an elderly priest called Cruithnechan, who is described as his 'foster-father'. As we have already observed, this was not an uncommon experience for a son of the nobility. In his case it seems to have led to an early decision to devote himself to the dedicated Christian life and become a monk. Later and less reliable sources tell of him learning the alphabet by eating shaped biscuits and remembering the one hundredth psalm when his ancient teacher forgot it. Subsequently he seems to have studied at a monastery in Leinster, which had one of the best-established church schools in the first half of the sixth century, and possibly also at Moville. The *Irish Life* of Columba, possibly composed around 1150, states that he completed his training under another Finnian at Clonard and, having been ordained presbyter, joined a monastic community near Dublin. After a plague there, he apparently returned to his own Cenél Conaill people in Ulster where he may have founded some small monastic communities. Later sources claim that he set up some three hundred monasteries in Ireland before his departure for Iona, including the communities at Derry, Raphoe, Durrow, Kells, Lambay and Moone, but this is generally dismissed by historians as without any historical basis. The truth is that we do not really know where Columba was based or what he was doing before he made his fateful journey from Donegal in 563. What we do know is that he was an exceedingly well-connected churchman who had something of the qualities of both the fox and the dove in his complex character.

Notes

1   Alfred Smyth, *Warlords and Holy Men* (Edward Arnold, London, 1984), p.9

2   *Life of St Columba*, written by Adomnán and translated by William Reeves (Edmonston & Douglas, Edinburgh, 1874) p.103

3   Thomas Charles-Edwards, 'The social background to Irish peregrinatio' in *Celtica*, no.11 (1976), p.56

4   On this important group of Christians, whose influence on Irish monasticism was very considerable, see *The Lives of the Desert Fathers* introduced by Benedicta Ward and translated by Norman Russell (Mowbray, Oxford, 1981)

5   Thomas Clancy and Gilbert Márkus, *IONA: The Earliest Poetry of a Celtic Monastery* (Edinburgh University Press, Edinburgh, 1995), p.147

6   *Ibid.*, p.136

7   *Life of Columba*, p.80. Richard Sharpe discusses the placing of this statement in Adomnán's original text in note 356 to his edition of the *Life of Columba* (Penguin Books, Harmondsworth, 1995), pp.353-4

8   Máire Herbert, *Iona, Kells and Derry* (Clarendon Press, Oxford, 1988), p.28

9   Tim Clarkson, *Columba* (Birlinn, Edinburgh, 2012), p.48

10 *Warlords and Holy Men*, p.100

11 Clarkson, *Columba*, p.56

12 Mary Donaldson, *Further Wanderings – Mainly in Argyll* (Alexander Gardner, Paisley, 1926), p.7

13 This hymn can be found in the *Hymnal for Scotland* (Oxford University Press, 1950). The late Betty Hannah, widow of the author, kindly gave me permission to quote it.

14 Ian Finlay, *Columba* (Victor Gollancz, London, 1979), p.187

15 Clancy & Márkus, *IONA*, p.113

16 John Ryan, *Irish Monasticism* (Four Courts Press, Dublin, 1992), p.91

Two

Columba the kingmaker
and church-planter

Two activities dominate Columba's public life as a church leader as it is portrayed in the earliest surviving accounts – forging relationships with kings and establishing a network of churches and monasteries. The prominence of these two themes in early sources may throw more light on the preoccupations of Columba's biographers in the century or so following his death than on the saint's own priorities. Recent scholarship has clearly demonstrated that Adomnán deliberately cast his subject in the role of the Old Testament figure of Samuel and emphasised Columba's kingmaking activities in order to support the claim of later Iona abbots to consecrate the kings of Dál Riata. It is also clear that the twelfth-century *Irish Life* portrayed him as setting up numerous monastic foundations in Ireland as part of its attempt to assert the primacy of Derry in the Columban *familia*. Yet even allowing for exaggeration and special pleading on the part of his early biographers, it is impossible to ignore the considerable evidence they provide that both kingmaking and church-planting ranked high on Columba's own agenda.

If these seem somewhat incompatible occupations, then we are brought back to the tension that we have already identified within Columba's personality. The gentle, scholarly monk who periodically retreated to his cell and spent the night reciting psalms on the sea shore was also the high-born friend of kings who involved himself in political affairs. The man of God was also a man of action. Columba's deep commitment to following Christ and to the monastic and priestly vocation did not efface his loyalty and blood-ties to his Uí Néill and Cenél Conaill kinsmen. Nor did it quell his fascination with the dynastic disputes of the day. Adomnán's *Life* is full of prophecies about the outcome of battles and predictions as to who would succeed to a particular kingship. Although several may not be genuine, it is difficult to dismiss them all and to avoid the impression that they give of a man whose life had two distinct foci – the one spiritual and centred on the institution of the monastery, the other secular and centred on the institution of kingship.

In fact, these two themes were more compatible and intertwined than might at first sight appear. Columba almost certainly used his royal connections to forward the cause of Christianity and to win powerful support and patronage for the church. He also seems to have been more than happy to provide Christian legitimation for kingship and to offer prayer and protection both to his royal kinsmen and to other princes and monarchs. The way in which he bound the two relatively new institutions of church and monarchy together was to have profound and positive implications for the future development of both and for the order and stability of early medieval British society. In the opinion of the distinguished modern historian of early Ireland Máire Herbert, 'overall, perhaps the most important aspect of the achievement of Colum Cille was the fact that he bridged the divide between secular and ecclesiastic realms of interest. More than that, his career may be seen to have shown the potential for mutual benefit arising out of co-operation between church and dynasty'.[1]

Columba lived at a time of transition when the anarchy of a society dominated by tribal warlords was giving way to a more peaceful and settled system of government based on rule by a number of royal dynasties. This movement towards greater order was both paralleled and helped by the development of monastic confederations or families which often enjoyed close relations with the emerging royal households and shared their territorial boundaries. The Columban *familia*, which consisted of the monasteries founded both by Columba himself and by his successors, was to become the biggest and most influential of these confederations, its fortunes closely linked with those of both the Northern Irish Uí Néill and the rulers of Scots Dál Riata.

The close connection between the development of the institutions of church and monarchy in the period from the sixth to the tenth century is important to understanding the nature of Christianity in the Celtic realms of the British Isles. It made a significant mark on the poems and prayers of the time which often took up the language and imagery of kingship in their depiction of God and Christ. A notable example occurs in the eighth-century Irish poem '*Rob tu mo bhiole, a Comdi cride*', known to us through its early twentieth-century translation and versification as the hymn 'Be Thou My Vision' which twice refers to God as 'the High King of Heaven'. It was not just in Celtic Britain, of course, that kingship and Christianity progressed together and that royal patronage helped the cause of the church. The apparent conversion of the Emperor Constantine in 312 AD and the subsequent promotion of Christianity as the favoured religion in the Roman Empire had led to a great increase in church-building and ecclesiastical wealth and influence in continental Europe, perhaps at the expense of the integrity and simplicity associated with the earlier followers of Jesus. Within the British Isles there seems to have been less ostentatious building up of ecclesiastical establishments. That is not to say, however, that the support and patronage of secular rulers was any less important to the church. An appreciation of this fact was no doubt partly what made Columba so keen not just to keep in with kings but to help them on their way.

The way in which Columba built up close relations with rulers is highlighted in the friendship which he apparently established soon after his arrival from Ireland with the king of Scots Dál Riata, Conall mac Comgaill. As we have already noted, it may well be that Columba made Conall's stronghold at Dunadd on the Kintyre peninsula his first port of call and that the king subsequently gave him the island of Iona for his monastic foundation. There are also grounds for thinking that Columba's Uí Néill relatives may have

encouraged him to go and settle in Scots Dál Riata in order to promote an alliance with the rulers of this potentially powerful new
kingdom. Whatever its origins, there is no doubt that the close
relationship forged between Columba and Conall proved mutually
beneficial to their successors. It ensured royal patronage and protection for the church centred on Iona while greatly enhancing
the prestige and legitimacy of the new Irish kingdom in Scotland.
For the next two hundred years or more the fortunes of the Columban monastic *familia* and the royal house of Dál Riata were
inextricably intertwined.

There is an interesting confirmation of the closeness of this
link and an intriguing glimpse of Columba as kingmaker in Dál
Riata in the one surviving fragment of the life of him written by
Cumméne, the seventh abbot of Iona, in the 630s or 640s. It tells
of the saint promising the kingship to Conall's cousin, Aedán mac
Gabhráin, and his descendants on condition that they are loyal to
his successors as abbots of Iona and his royal kinsmen in Ireland.
In his slightly later *Life* Adomnán devotes a chapter to this episode, describing an angel of the Lord visiting Columba when he
was on the island of Hinba and commanding him to ordain Aedán
as king. He is at first reluctant to follow this order, preferring
Aedán's brother Eoganán, but the angel strikes him with a whip
(the origin, according to Adomnán, of the scar which remains
with him for the rest of his life) and returns on three successive
nights to repeat the demand that Aedán must be ordained king, a
ceremony which Columba duly carries out on his return to Iona
where he finds Aedán waiting for him.

Adomnán's description of what appears to be a fully-developed
royal anointing ritual is the first of its kind in European literature
and has led some historians to suggest that the first recorded
Christian ordination of a king anywhere in Europe took place on
Iona in 574. A monograph by Michael Enright has, however, cast

doubt on the historicity of this event and suggests that the episode of Aedán's ordination may have been invented by Adomnán and inserted in his *Life of Columba* in order to bolster the concept of Christian kingship in general and more specifically to support the claim of the abbots of Iona to consecrate the kings of Dál Riata.[2] It is certainly true that Adomnán makes much of Columba's role in choosing as well as anointing the rulers of Dál Riata. He is portrayed as picking out under divine inspiration both Aedán and his successor Eochaid Buide. Both Enright and Richard Sharpe, editor of the latest edition of Adomnán's *Life*, agree that the chapter which describes Columba choosing Eochaid Buide is directly based on the Old Testament story of Samuel choosing David to replace King Saul.[3] It may well be that Adomnán over-emphasised Columba's kingmaking activities for his own purposes and projected back an arrangement which had only developed in his own time whereby the abbots of Iona consecrated the rulers of Dál Riata in order to give them greater authority and tradition. This should not, however, lead us to lose sight of the importance of the link between the spread of Christianity and the legitimisation of kingship in Celtic society, nor of the key role that Columba's successors on Iona, if not he himself, played in strengthening that link.

Columba's apparent close interest in the fortunes of kings and princes was not just confined to those in his adopted Scottish homeland. He also continued to maintain close contact with his royal relations back in Ireland. Indeed, he may well have been the moving spirit behind a convention held at Druim Ceat near Derry in 575 which brought together the northern Uí Néill and the rulers of Scots Dál Riata. The leading representatives of each group, Aed mac Ainmirech, King of Cenél Conaill, and Aedán mac Gabráin, King of Dál Riata, were both figures with whom he had very close connections. Columba himself was apparently present at this gathering which seems to have cemented the alliance between these two powerful dynasties and had the effect of making Scots Dál Riata independent of its Irish counterpart. According to the poet Dallán Forgaill, the saint came to the convention more in the guise of a Celtic chieftain than a humble monk, bringing with him a retinue of forty priests, twenty bishops, fifty deacons and thirty students. Ian Finlay comments: 'As a Celtic prince, he would be aware that a meek appearance would count for nothing and that he must present himself with a semblance of the trappings of royalty.'[4]

There is also evidence that Columba made it his business to forge good relations with the kings of the principal peoples who occupied the Scottish mainland in the sixth century. As in Ireland, this was an important period of transition in which the anarchy and territorial warfare that had followed the departure of the Romans around 400 AD gave way to a more settled situation where what would eventually become Scotland was split into four separate kingdoms. While the Irish (known by their Roman name of *Scoti*) increasingly dominated Argyll and the Inner and Outer Hebrides, south west and west central Scotland were inhabited by the Strathclyde Britons, whose king was based in Dumbarton. The Highlands, the north east and east central Scotland was the heartland of the Picts, whose high king ruled from Inverness. The Lothians and Borders were part of the Anglian kingdom of Bernicia and were effectively ruled by the kings of Northumbria.

Columba seems to have had dealings with the rulers of all four of these kingdoms which would eventually be brought together under a single monarch to form the modern nation of Scotland. He was naturally closest to the kings of Dál Riata who were of Irish ancestry like himself, in alliance with his own Uí Néill kinsmen and in control of the area where he established his monasteries. He is also portrayed as being on cordial terms with Roderc, king of the Strathclyde Britons, who seems to have been a Christian. Although there is no direct evidence of contact with the rulers of Bernicia, the fact that two Northumbrian princes fled to Iona for sanctuary in 616 suggests that relations between the Columban *familia* and the Northumbrian royal family must have been established either during the saint's lifetime or very shortly after it.

Perhaps the most interesting and also the most inscrutable of Columba's royal relationships was that with Brude, the Pictish king. The sources are frankly conflicting here. Bede seems to suggest that Columba converted the pagan king to Christianity eight years after he had become ruler of his people (i.e. in 566) and that it was as a consequence of this conversion that Brude granted the saint the island of Iona which was under Pictish control. This, however, seems a less likely account of their dealings than that contained in Adomnán's *Life* which describes at least one encounter between the two men at Brude's stronghold near Inverness but makes no claim that the pagan king was converted to Christianity. Indeed, Adomnán does not portray Columba as setting out to convert Brude or the Picts and gives a much more limited purpose to the saint's journey through the Great Glen to confer with the pagan king, suggesting that its primary and relatively limited objective was to secure royal protection and safety for a group of monks from Iona who were living as hermits on Orkney. It is also possible that there may have been a political agenda behind the meeting of Columba and Brude with the Pictish king being keen to secure an alliance with the Dál Riata Scots at a time when he was anxious about the rising power of the Anglian kingdom of Northumbria.

Were Columba's dealings with kings and princes motivated by his penchant for mixing with monarchs and political parleying and his enthusiasm for the institution of kingship or by his evangelistic zeal and desire to open up new mission fields for the Iona monks?

Behind this question lies the much bigger issue of whether Columba was primarily an ecclesiastical administrator or a missionary. Were the last three decades of his life spent largely on Iona building up and administering the monastery and its satellites or were they rather filled with preaching tours and missionary journeys around Scotland and perhaps even further afield?

Once again, the evidence is conflicting. Some sources portray Columba as largely remaining on Iona and dividing his time between priestly and pastoral duties, scholarly pursuits and the leadership of the monastic community. This is broadly the picture given by Adomnán although his *Life* records the saint making frequent visits to Hinba, possibly for regular periods of solitary retreat, and occasional visits to Skye and Ardnamurchan. On at least one occasion Adomnán describes Columba as journeying to the other side of Druim Alban ('the Spine of Scotland', thought to refer to the Grampian Mountains) and being among the Picts. There is, in fact, considerable debate among scholars as to how many journeys into Pictish territory Adomnán reports Columba as making. Some are inclined to put the number as high as seven although Marjorie Anderson, editor of an important edition of Adomnán's *Life* which came out in 1961, took the view that all of his accounts relate to one single expedition made up the Great Glen to Brude's court. Although Adomnán describes a number of individual conversions secured by Columba on his travels, the primary impression he gives is not of missionary activity and certainly not of mass evangelism.

Other sources make much more of Columba's missionary endeavours and portray him as being constantly on the move, converting the heathen people of North Britain. The *Irish Life* perhaps conveys this impression most strongly: 'When Colum Cille had founded Iona he went on a preaching circuit among the Scots and Britons and Saxons, and converted them to faith and belief after he had performed many miracles and raised the dead to life.'[5] The *Amra Choluimb Chille* suggests more specifically that his main missionary field lay among the Picts in central and eastern Scotland (modern Angus and Perthshire), describing him as 'the teacher who would teach the tribes of the Tay' and commenting that: His blessing turned them, the mouth of the fierce ones who lived on the Tay, to the will of the king.[6]

The most quoted passage about Columba's missionary activities, and its antecedents, comes from Bede's *Ecclesiastical History*:

> *In the year of our Lord 565, there came into Britain from Ireland a famous priest and abbot, marked as a monk by habit and manner of life, whose name was Columba, to preach the word of God to the provinces of the northern Picts, who are separated from the southern parts belonging to that nation by steep and rugged mountains. For the southern Picts, who dwell on this side of those mountains, had, it is said, long before forsaken the errors of idolatry, and received the true faith by the preaching of Bishop Ninian, a most reverend and holy man of the British nation, who had been regularly instructed at Rome in the faith and mysteries of the truth; whose episcopal see, named after St Martin the bishop, and famous for a church dedicated to him (wherein Ninian himself and many other saints rest in the body), is now in the possession of the English nation. The place belongs to the province of the Bernicians, and is commonly called the White House, because he there built a church of stone, which was not usual among the Britons.[7]*

Bede's words, which were written at least one hundred years after Columba's death, have been highly influential in determining the popular impression of how Scotland was evangelised. They suggest that Columba was responsible for bringing Christianity to the northern Picts – those living in the northern and western Highlands and in Aberdeenshire north of the Mounth (the upland ridge which skirts the Dee Valley from Lochnagar to Aberdeen) – the southern Picts, inhabiting Perthshire, Angus, Fife and the lands around the Forth, having earlier been converted by Ninian, a shadowy figure for whom our only sources, apart from Bede, are an eighth-century poem and a twelfth-century *Life* by Ailred of Rievaulx. As a result of Bede's account, for many centuries Columba and Ninian posthumously vied for the accolade of being hailed as the true apostle of Scotland. Scholars championed one or the other in a somewhat unedifying academic wrangle which often owed more to sectarian and ethnic prejudices than to the interests of historical truth. Columba tended to find favour with enthusiasts for the Gaelic language and all things Celtic and Irish. Ninian's champions, on the other hand, were drawn particularly from those wanting to emphasise the Britishness of the Galloway saint and the indigenous nature of early missionary activity in Scotland.

The debate over which saint should be seen as the principal evangelist of Scotland was particularly lively in the early decades of last century. Leading the pro-Columban camp was William Watson, Professor of Celtic at Edinburgh University, who underlined the Irish contribution to the Christianising of Scotland and enthusiastically followed Bede in crediting the conversion of the northern Picts to Columba. Ranged against him were a trio of Protestant scholars: Frank Knight, United Free Church minister and keen archaeologist, Archibald Scott, Church of Scotland minister in Kildonan (Helmsdale) and Dr Douglas Simpson, librarian of the University of Aberdeen. Knight pointed to the large number of evangelists active in Scotland prior to Columba. Scott was in no doubt as to the primacy of 'Ninian the Great' over Columba and regarded the 'great mission' undertaken by the Briton as the key event in the early Christian history of Scotland, leading directly to the establishment of what was to remain the sole church of the Picts until the time of Kenneth MacAlpin in the mid-ninth century.[8] Douglas Simpson was even more enthusiastic in his championship of Ninian and his dismissal of Columba. Holding that the Irish saint's political activities were 'consistently directed against the Pictish king and people', he held that 'long before Columba's time, Christianity was widely spread among the Picts'.[9] The key agent of this early evangelisation of Highland and northern Scotland had to be Ninian. On the basis of church dedications, Simpson argued that the British saint had travelled from Galloway via Glasgow and Stirling to Dunottar and Methlick in the north east and Glenurquhart in the Highlands. In his view, indeed, Ninian had got as far north as Caithness and Shetland.

More recent and less partisan scholarship has seriously challenged, if not completely exploded, the arguments of Scott and Simpson and suggested a much more limited role for Ninian. The late Charles Thomas, a leading authority on Christianity in Britain in the period between 300 and 700, cast grave doubts on Simpson's assertions about the extent of Ninian's travels by demonstrating that many of the church dedications which he took to be contemporary were in fact made several centuries after the saint's death.[10] John MacQueen, former director of the School of Scottish Studies at Edinburgh University, has argued that Ninian was largely active in the areas of Dumfries, Bernicia (the Borders) and possibly in Renfrewshire and Stirling and that he did not penetrate significantly into areas occupied by the Picts.[11] Archaeological finds tend to support this theory, providing no evidence for Christianity among the Picts until the sixth century at the very earliest.

The dating of Ninian and the nature of the church with which he was involved have also been the subject of considerable controversy over the last few years. There is uncertainty as to how soon after the departure of the Romans from Britain he appeared on the scene and whether the church in Galloway of which he appears to have been a bishop, with its centre at Whithorn, was a surviving offshoot of Roman Christianity, possibly linked to ecclesiastical centres further south such as Carlisle or even York, or an early example of indigenous British Christianity.

We know from archaeological evidence that a Christian settlement existed at Whithorn at least from the mid-fifth century, making it an earlier ecclesiastical and monastic site than Iona. The Latinus stone found there, which apparently marks the grave of a father and daughter, can be dated to this period and is, in fact, the earliest Christian memorial in Scotland. What is not clear, even from Bede's account, is whether Ninian actually founded the church at Whithorn, or how long before Columba he lived. Previously it was thought that Ninian was a contemporary of Martin of Tours, the Hungarian-born saint who brought Eastern monasticism to the West and who died in 397. This date was traditionally taken for the foundation of Whithorn, largely on the basis of a remark in Ailred's *Life* that news came through of Martin's death as the church there was being built. This gave rise to the idea that Ninian had visited St Martin's monastery in Gaul on the way back from his training and ordination in Rome and dedicated his own monastic foundation to him when he returned to his native Galloway in the last days of Roman occupation of Britain.

Modern scholars are almost all of the view that this is too early a dating for Ninian. John MacQueen places him in the first half of the fifth century while still holding on to the traditional view that he founded the church at Whithorn. The Glasgow-based scholar Alan Macquarrie argues for an even later dating and maintains

that Ninian almost certainly belonged to the first half of the sixth
century and overlapped with Columba. In his view, Whithorn was
already a thriving monastery and Christian centre when Ninian,
who had been born around 493 from the same British Christian
stock as Patrick, went there to train. He possibly travelled to
Rome, coming back to Britain as a missionary bishop working predominantly south of the Forth, notably in the Borders area around
Peebles. Possibly he later returned to Whithorn as bishop of Galloway, rebuilding the church there and dedicating it to St Martin
of Tours, whose cult seems to have been strong among north
British Christians. Several early sources mention Ninian as coming
into conflict with Tudwal, a king of Dumbarton, whose reign Macquarrie reckons can be dated fairly accurately to the mid-sixth
century. On this interpretation, Ninian died around 563, just thirty
years or so before Columba. Like Dr MacQueen and other modern
scholars, Dr Macquarrie is convinced that Ninian did not venture
beyond southern Scotland. If he did do any preaching or evangelistic work among the Pictish people, then it was with an extreme
southern offshoot who lived south of the Forth.[12]

If this recent work somewhat diminishes the importance and
primacy of Ninian, it does not necessarily establish Columba as
the unchallenged apostle of Scotland and chief evangelist of the
Picts. Rather it places both men in the context of a more gradual
and fragmented process of Christianisation in which many others
also took part. The Ninian versus Columba debate has at least produced one beneficial result in reminding us that there were two
different movements at work bringing Christianity to seventh-century Scotland. The older one came from the British church,
centred possibly on Carlisle and with its missionary base in Strathclyde, sending missionaries westwards into Dumfries and Galloway, eastwards into the Northumbrian-controlled Lothians,
northwards towards Stirling and possibly also into the Pictish

lands of Perthshire and Fife. The later missionary movement came in the wake of the Irish push into western Scotland and spread from its base in Dál Riata eastwards into the central Highlands and Tayside and north into the Highlands and the north east. Place names can give us much information as to the progress of these two movements. Names with *eccles* (deriving from the Latin *ecclesia* and the British *eglwys*) suggest early Christian churches founded under British influence. They are found in considerable numbers across southern Scotland, with a particular concentration in the south west, and up the east coast between the Forth and the Mounth but are hardly found north of the Mounth or west of the Great Glen. Other place names give evidence of early Irish penetration – a good example is Atholl in north Perthshire which derives from *Ath Flhóda*, meaning 'a second Ireland'.

The extent to which these two movements had their early head-quarters at Whithorn and Iona respectively is by no means certain. Although Bede states that the monastery on Iona 'was for a long time the chief of almost all those of the northern Scots, and all those of the Picts', there is little evidence that Columba himself planted any monastic communities or churches in the Pictish regions of Perthshire, the Highlands and the north and north east.[13] Bede's remarks probably apply to the period a hundred years or more after Columba's death when his followers had established communities in Pictish territory and possibly also when churches founded by missionaries not directly associated with Iona had become absorbed into the increasingly powerful Columban *familia*.

It may well be, in fact, that there was a third important move-ment bringing Christianity to the Picts in the late sixth and early seventh centuries quite independent of the British mission from Whithorn and the Irish mission from Iona. The conversion of those who lived in the region of the Tay may have been brought about by monks and nuns based at Abernethy between Perth and

Newburgh near the present border between Perthshire and Fife. The origins of the monastery there, from which the fine round tower still survives, are shrouded in mystery and it is not clear whether it was founded by British or Irish evangelists, or even as an indigenous Pictish initiative. Three of the lists of Pictish kings assign the foundation of Abernethy to 463, which would conceivably make it earlier than both Whithorn and Iona, but others put it later. Most scholars are inclined to opt for a date during the reign of either Gartnait, who died around 601, or Nechtan, who ruled in the 620s. This later dating is probably the most likely. There is a tradition that Nechtan founded a church dedicated to St Brigit at Abernethy in the presence of Darlugdach, abbess of Kildare. Alfred Smyth has suggested that this community may have originally been established with Irish nuns from Kildare around 625. Whenever it was founded, and whether its first members were Irish, British or Picts, there is no doubt that the monastery at Abernethy played an important role in the evangelisation of Perthshire, Fife and Tayside from at least the early seventh century onwards. I have heard it argued very emphatically that Abernethy rather than Iona should be regarded as the true cradle of Christianity in Scotland but that is not a claim which I think I had better pursue in a book commemorating Columba and published by the Iona Community!

What is absolutely clear is that Columba was by no means the only Christian missionary to be active in the vast areas of central and northern Scotland occupied by the Picts in the sixth century. Nor was he the first to penetrate these pagan realms. In his seminal two-volume study of the archaeological evidence for the early Christianising of Scotland, Frank Knight identified eighty men and women who were actively evangelising the country before Columba had left his native Ireland and 'who had literally covered the land with hundreds of churches before the Iona mission began'.[14] It is difficult to avoid the conclusion that had they been fortunate enough to have royal blood, find a biographer like Adomnán, and forge close links with the family that was to provide Scotland with its ruling dynasty, they too might have become famous names.

Among these early pioneers were several near-contemporaries of Columba who came from Ireland, and established monasteries in Dál Riata. St Catan, St Moluag and St Blane all hailed from the monastery at Bangor in County Down. Catan founded a community at Kilchattan Bay at the south end of Bute and was possibly also associated with foundations on Colonsay, Islay and Jura. Moluag founded an important monastery at Lismore before working in the Hebrides, notably on Skye and Tiree, and then moving to the north east mainland, where he died possibly at Rosemarkie in Ross-shire in 592. Blane is traditionally credited with establishing the church at Dunblane after first setting up a monastery at Kingarth on Bute. According to some accounts St Machar, associated with preaching to the Picts of Aberdeenshire and founding the church and city of Aberdeen, was one of Columba's original companions on his journey from Donegal. Another of his original companions, if an equally unlikely story is to be believed, was St Donnan, who seems to have evangelised much of Skye and who became one of the first Christian martyrs in Scotland when Pictish raiders massacred all 150 members of the community that he had established on the island of Eigg in 617.

Curiously, Adomnán makes no reference in his *Life* to any of these Irish monks despite the fact that they were apparently living and working so close to Iona. However, he does refer to Columba's friendship with a number of others who seem to have been operating quite independently of Iona and its daughter foundations. In one chapter he describes four saints who had founded monasteries in Ireland visiting Columba on Hinba. Significantly, two of them seem also to have established monastic communities in

Scotland although Adomnán does not mention these, presumably out of a concern not to detract from the primacy of the Columban *familia*. St Comgall of Bangor seems to have set up a monastery on Tiree and St Brendan of Clonfert one at Eileach an Naoimh in the Garvellochs in the mouth of the Firth of Lorne. The other two Irish saints described by Adomnán as visiting Hinba were St Cainnech of Aghaboe, who is credited with being the first evangelist to the Picts of North East Fife in the area around Kinrymonth, later known as St Andrews, and St Cormac, who is also portrayed by Adomnán as being commended by Columba to King Brude and voyaging to Orkney. This reference has led some scholars to suggest that Columba 'sub-contracted' evangelistic work among the Picts, especially those in the northern isles, to Cormac.

A number of other Irish and British monks were also preaching to the Picts during Columba's lifetime. They included St Kessog, who supposedly evangelised the Trossachs from his base on Monk's Island in Loch Lomond, and St Serf who seems to have been active in the Ochil hills and Fife and had a similar island retreat on Loch Leven. St Ternan, a shadowy figure possibly based at Abernethy, is associated with the Christianising of the Dee valley in Aberdeenshire. St Columba's best-known evangelist contemporary, the British-born St Kentigern, also known as Mungo, is traditionally portrayed as the first bishop of the Strathclyde Britons. He did most of his missionary work in Strathclyde although an almost certainly fabricated story in Jocelyn's twelfth-century *Life* describes him meeting Columba near the banks of the Tay. There were undoubtedly many other monks whose pioneering work in bringing Christianity to the remoter parts of Scotland has gone unsung while their better-connected contemporary continues to receive honour and attention. Alexander McBain, a scholar of the Gaelic language, noted more than a hundred years ago that Columba 'swallowed up into his own fame all the work of his predecessors, companions and contemporaries, and deprived generations of pioneers and missionaries of their just fame'.[15] There are stories in Adomnán's *Life* describing Columba travelling some distance away from Iona but they do not, on the whole, suggest large-scale evangelism or missionary endeavour. One, set in the 'rough and rocky' district of Ardnamurchan, describes the saint miraculously creating a spring of water and font in which to baptise a child brought to him. This is supposedly the origin of what is still called Columba's Well, a natural basin into which water drips in a cave known as Uamha Thuill near Kilmory on the north Ardnamurchan coast. It was renowned for its healing properties and resorted to by people suffering from mental illness until the mid-nineteenth century. Another story set in this area tells of him standing in the sea praying and causing a storm which drowns an evil man. This is said to have taken place in 'Sharp Bay' which has been tentatively identified as Sanna Bay at the west end of the Ardnamurchan peninsula. Adomnán also suggests that Columba twice got as far as the boundary between Ardnamurchan and Moidart, the northernmost point of Argyll, in his search for good oak timber for building his monastery on Iona. On one of these visits he was delighted to find the river where he and his companions halted teeming with salmon. According to local folklore, he used the word 'sale' to describe the fish, thus originating the name 'Shiel' by which the river has been known ever since.

Adomnán does describe Columba occasionally venturing further afield into Pictish territory, as in his visit to Skye where he struck dead a wild boar, and his journey up the Great Glen to Inverness to see King Brude. His ability to tame the Loch Ness Monster, whom he encountered on this latter journey and prevented from gobbling up one of his monks, does seem to have inspired the local 'heathen natives' who witnessed it to 'magnify the God of the Christians' but on the whole these occasional excursions beyond Dál Riata are not portrayed as being primarily evangelistic in purpose. I agree with Tim Clarkson's assessment of Columba's travels in Pictland: 'We glean no sense of a formal Christianising "mission", still less the great achievements envisaged by Bede. Columba's gains at the expense of Pictish paganism seem to have been token successes involving a few high-status converts. The wider populace apparently remained unbaptised.'[16]

It certainly seems on the basis of the best available evidence we now have that Columba does not deserve the accolade of apostle to the Picts. His forays into Pictish territory seem to have been few and far between and it is doubtful whether he felt any strong evangelistic impulse to convert this particular people to Christianity. Instead his missionary efforts, such as they were, seem to have been concentrated very largely among his fellow *Scoti* in Dál Riata. Although Adomnán describes him as founding monasteries on both sides of Druim Alban, i.e. among the Irish and the Picts, there is no evidence of any Columban foundations in areas occupied by the Picts and all those that we know of are either in Scots Dál Riata or Ireland. Significant evangelism of the Picts almost certainly did not come until the seventh century when it was undertaken by such figures as St Maelrubha, a possible relative of Columba who lived from c.642 to 722 and made a series of journeys from his base at Applecross into Inverness-shire, Banffshire, Skye and Harris, and as far north as Cape Wrath. Archaeological evidence suggesting that the area around the Moray Firth was not converted to Christianity until the late seventh or early eighth century would certainly tend to favour Maelrubha, rather than his better known predecessor from Iona, as the true evangelist of the northern Picts.

How then should Columba's part in the story of the Christianising of the British Isles be assessed? Perhaps we should follow his early biographers and regard him less as a missionary or evangelist and more as a planter of churches. This is certainly how Adomnán saw him. In the second preface to his *Life* he describes Columba as 'the father and founder of monasteries'. The elegy that appeared a few years after his death refers to him as *cét cell custóit* (the guardian of a hundred churches). This was almost certainly a considerable exaggeration but there seems little doubt that he was personally responsible for founding a number of monasteries, including several in Ireland before his departure from there in 563. He is widely credited with establishing a monastery at Derry, which may well have served as a port of communication between Iona and other monasteries in the Columban *familia* in Ulster. He also seems to have returned from Iona to Ireland to found a monastery at Durrow around 587. In Scotland, Columba's church-planting activities involved the foundation of several monasteries across Argyll. Like their Iona mother house, most of them were located on islands and all were located within the kingdom of Dál Riata. Adomnán mentions two monasteries on Tiree – one at Artchain and the other at Mag Luinge, which was probably situated at Soroby on the south-east of the island and seems to have been set up as a penitents' colony to which Columba sent those who came to him seeking pastoral counselling and absolution for the crimes that they had committed. There are also references to him founding monasteries on the unidentified islands of Elen and Hinba, and building a chapel on the tiny island of Bernera off Lismore where he sometimes prayed under a yew tree. The only mainland monastic foundation mentioned by Adomnán is that of *Cella Diuni* on the shores of Loch Awe. There is no consensus among historians as to where this was. Tom Clancy favours a site near Kilchrenan at the north end of the loch while both Marion Campbell and Marian Pallister prefer Kilneuair, 'the Church of the Yews', which sits on a flat-topped knoll on the south east bank of Loch Awe close to an old drove road to Loch Fyne. It was known

at least as far back as 1389 as 'SanctColmysKirke in Glasrie'. There
have also been suggestions that *Cella Diuni* may have been sited
at Kilmaha, roughly half way up the west side of Loch Awe, where
there is a chapel and burial ground.[17]

Ian Finlay commented in his biography of the saint that 'monasteries seem to spring up and bloom like flowers in the footsteps
of Columba, as though he created them with a wave of his bachuil;
but we know that in the first place he had to negotiate with the
king of the tribe for the grant of the land on which to build his
"city", then for endowments with which to launch and maintain
it.'[18] Here is a link between the two main activities which seemed
to occupy Columba's public life, at least if his early biographers
are to be believed. There are other connections between his kingmaking and church-planting activities. He ran his monastic *familia*
as though it was a kingdom, bound together by ties of kinship,
and ruled over by a dynasty with himself as the high king and his
relatives in charge of the subsidiary monasteries. His uncle was
abbot of the monastery on Hinba, his first cousin was abbot of one
of the monasteries on Tiree and the son of another cousin was
abbot of Durrow. Significantly, in the century after his death all
but one of the abbots of Iona, who exercised overlordship over the
entire Columban *familia*, were close blood relations of the founder.
In the words of Máire Herbert: 'The manner in which Colum Cille
organised the government of his monastic foundations would
seem to have been based on established secular concepts of overlordship, kinship and inheritance, so that the system had an in-
built potential for survival and continuity in Irish society.'[19]

As abbot of Iona Columba behaved very much like an Irish
high king. Although assiduous in caring for the souls and bodies
of the members of his own monastic *familia*, the evidence suggests
that he could also be fiercely autocratic and jealously territorial
when it came to dealing with those outside it. He seems, for

example, to have sought to prevent monks from Whithorn from setting up a community in the Hebrides, regarding such a move as an unwarrantable intrusion into his own sphere of influence. His authority derived as much, if not more, from his own personal charisma and leadership qualities than from his office. This reflects William Leask's dictum that 'the Celtic race is prone to follow leaders and not institutions'.[20] It was also undoubtedly helped by the significant power that abbots were coming to wield in the Irish church, itself another consequence of the close link between the spread of Christianity and the development of kingship. As Kathleen Hughes, a historian of early Irish Christianity, has written, 'The bishop stood in a similar relationship to his diocese as did the petty king to his *túath*; but the head of a great monastic *paruchia* was like a king over kings.'[21]

The word 'family' suggests close ties of kinship, loyalty, community and solidarity. It is significant that the Irish word for family is *muintir* which derives from the Latin *monasterium*. For Columba both the individual monastic community and the wider monastic federation were first and foremost families over which he presided as a benevolent, if firm, founding father. The same was true of the *túath* ruled by a just and kindly king. In his kingmaking and his church-planting, Columba was seeking to bring the order, stability and community of family life into the political and religious spheres. In place of the arbitrary rule of warlords and chieftains, he championed a new kind of authority in which the exercise of legitimate power and strength was tempered and complemented by the Christian virtues of justice, humility and mercy. These are the very qualities which, by all accounts, he brought to the oversight of the monasteries which made up his own extended family and which formed a kingdom which was firmly rooted in this world and yet also pointed to the world beyond.

Notes

1   Máire Herbert, *Iona, Kells and Derry*, p. 35

2   Michael Enright, *Iona, Tara and Soissons: The Origins of the Royal Anointing Ritual* (Waiter de Gruyter, Berlin, 1985)

3   See Richard Sharpe's note no. 358 in Penguin edition of *Life of Columba*, p.355

4   Ian Finlay, *Columba*, p.154

5   Máire Herbert, *Iona, Kells and Derry*, p.260

6   Thomas Clancy and Gilbert Márkus, IONA, pp.111, 113

7   *Bede's Ecclesiastical History of England*, trans. A.M. Sellar (George Bell, London, 1907), pp.141-2

8   Archibald Scott, *The Pictish Nation: Its People and Its Church* (T.N. Foulis, Edinburgh, 1918), p.1

9   W. Douglas Simpson, *The Historical Saint Columba* (Milne & Hutchison, Aberdeen, 1927), p.1

10   Charles Thomas, 'The Evidence for North Britain' in *Christianity in Britain, 300-700* edited by M.W. Barley and R.P.C. Hanson (Leicester University Press, Leicester, 1968), pp.94-116

11   John MacQueen, *St Nynia* (Polygon, Edinburgh, 1990)

12   Alan Macquarrie, 'The Date of St Ninian's Mission: A Reappraisal' in *Records of the Scottish Church History Society* vol.XXIII, Part 1 (1987)

13   *Bede's Ecclesiastical History of England*, p.140

14   G. Frank Knight, *Archaeological Light on the Early Christianising of Scotland* (James Clarke, London, 1933), p.7

15   Quoted in J.D. Galbraith, *St Machar's Cathedral: the Celtic Antecedents* (Friends of St Machar's Cathedral, Aberdeen, 1982), p.1

16   Tim Clarkson, *Columba*, p.142

17   Tom Clancy, 'Annat in Scotland and the Origins of the Parish', *Inness Review*, Vol.46, No.2, Autumn 1995, pp.91-115; Marion Campbell, *Argyll – The Enduring Heartland* (Kilmartin House Trust, 2001), p.150; Marian Pallister, *Argyll Curiorisities* (Birlinn, Edinburgh, 2007), p.4

18 Finlay, *Columba*, p.81
19 Máire Herbert, *Iona, Kells and Derry*, p.35
20 W.K. Leask, *Dr Thomas McLauchlan* (Oliphant, Anderson & Ferrier, Edinburgh, 1905), p.168
21 Kathleen Hughes, *The Church in Early Irish Society* (Methuen, London, 1966), p.74

Three

Columba the prophet, priest and poet

So far I have not mentioned the feature which dominates all the early writings about Columba – his sanctity as exemplified in a life filled with prophesying, miracle-working and heavenly visions. This aspect is particularly evident in Adomnán's *Life* which is almost wholly devoted to the saint's supernatural qualities, its three books covering respectively his prophetic revelations, his miracles of power and his visions of angels. His sanctity also figures prominently in the other major sources for Columba's life. The account written by Cumméne, seventh abbot of Iona, forty or so years after his illustrious predecessor's death, and now largely lost, was significantly entitled *The Book of the Miracles of Columba*. Descriptions of supernatural signs and wonders also abound in the poems and eulogies written about him in the seventh century by Dallán Forgaill and Beccán mac Luigdech.

This aspect of Columba's life, as it has been presented to us by his near contemporaries, causes considerable difficulties to the modern post-Enlightenment Protestant mind. The eighth Duke of Argyll, who was instrumental in restoring Iona Abbey in the 1890s and making it available once again for Christian worship on an ecumenical basis, found it impossible to cope with 'the atmosphere of miracle' pervading Adomnán's *Life* which he rejected as 'childish and utterly incredible'.[1] He was forced to the conclusion that the author had resorted to deliberate invention. Many other modern readers must have similar reactions as they encounter stories of the fearless and versatile saint taking on the Loch Ness monster, driving out a devil that was hiding at the bottom of a milk-pail and making a stone float in water like an apple.

Yet if we are to engage with and understand the culture which shaped Columba, and perhaps even more the outlook of those who followed him, we have to come to terms with a concept of sainthood which is very different from that which prevails today and which will strike many modern minds as primitive and credulous. As Thomas Clancy and Gilbert Márkus have commented, 'It is the belief in saints which separates, more than anything else, the medieval world from the classical world which preceded it, and the modern world which followed it.'[2] Nowadays, sainthood either has very technical connotations in terms of the various hoops through which those proposed for canonisation in the Roman Catholic Church have to jump, or else it is associated primarily with qualities of humility, gentleness, forbearance and kindness which make us say of someone that she or he is 'a real saint'. In Columba's day, not just in the Celtic world but throughout Christendom, it was part and parcel of a cult of holy men and women whose sanctity was demonstrated and proved as much by their ability to make prophecies and work miracles as by their inner qualities of discipline and self-sacrifice.

It is in this context that we need to approach the lives of Columba written by Cumméne and Adomnán and the poems by Dallán and Beccán. They stand in an early Christian tradition of *Vitae Sancti*, or saints' lives, which are essentially works of hagiography rather than biography, being designed to depict their subjects as exemplars of holiness and aiming not at historical accuracy and impartiality but at building up their readers' faith. Among the earliest and most important of these *Vitae* was Athanasius' *Life* of St Antony of Egypt, the pioneer desert father, and Sulpicius Severus' *Life* of St Martin of Tours, the figure who brought the principles of Eastern monasticism to the West. Both of these works heavily influenced Adomnán's treatment of the life of Columba and he quoted verbatim from the latter at a number of points in his own book.

The clearest influences on this particular genre of early Christian literature are the Gospel stories about the life and work of Jesus. The authors of the *Vitae Sancti* sought to establish the saintliness of their subjects by showing how closely they followed in the footsteps of their Lord. This involved portraying them as working miracles as well as taking up their own crosses and following the path of self-denial. Several of the wonders which Adomnán depicts Columba performing – turning water into wine, stilling a storm, raising a dead boy to life and driving out demons – directly parallel miracle stories in the Gospels. Others, such as the drawing of water from the side of a hard rock, recall episodes in the Old Testament. There are also clear biblical echoes in the 'Annunciation' passages found in all the early lives of Columba which describe the saint's birth being foretold by a series of signs and wonders.

There is another substantial clutch of miracles apparently performed by Columba which do not have such close biblical precedents. These involve him interacting with the indigenous pagan belief system of the people whom he meets on his forays into the Scottish mainland, particularly the Picts. The stories of his encounters with what anthropologists would call 'primal religion' fall into two broad categories. The first tell of the saint baptising a pagan shrine or symbol, usually by blessing it, with the result that it is 'converted' and Christianised. A good example of this is the episode recounted by Adomnán (Book 2, Chapter 11) involving the blessing of a well worshipped by the local people despite the fact that all who drank or washed at it were struck down by 'the devil's art' and left half blind, crippled or leprous. As a result of Columba's blessing, the well loses its old malevolent power and develops healing properties. The second group of stories show Columba actually taking on and out-gunning pagan wizards and sorcerers by practising more potent and spectacular magic than they do. Adomnán gives a good example in Book 2, Chapter 34 of his *Life* when he describes Columba dispersing a mist which the wizard Broichan had brought down to prevent him sailing up Loch Ness and then turning round a contrary wind conjured up by the wizard so that it is favourable and behind him. Adomnán also recounts a somewhat similar trial of strength taking place between Columba and the pagan advisers of Brude in the Pictish king's stronghold in a scene that is strongly reminiscent of the legendary encounter between St Patrick and Laogaire, the pagan high king of Ireland, on the sacred hill of Tara.

These stories point us to two important and in some ways contradictory aspects of the relationship between the new religion of Christianity and the old primal or pagan religion of the British Isles from the sixth century onwards. At one level, early Christian leaders like Columba seem to have sought to incorporate elements of the old faith by baptising or converting them. This was perhaps particularly the case with practices such as the worship of wells and other sacred places which could be blessed and brought within the Christian economy of salvation without too much difficulty. Yet at the same time Columba and his Christian contemporaries also seem to have confronted and taken on pagan priests and magicians. This is the clear message of the encounter with Broichan. There is a sense here of an almost tit-for-tat contest between the representatives of paganism and Christianity with each side seeking to show that they can work the bigger and better miracles. It is notable that nearly all of these contests are depicted as taking place in front of pagan audiences and are located in Pictland. Adomnán concludes his account of Columba's quelling of the Loch Ness monster, which apparently only had to hear his voice to recoil in terror, with the observation that 'even the barbarous heathens who were present were forced by the greatness of this miracle, which they themselves had seen, to magnify the God of the Christians.'[3] In similar vein he reports King Brude changing his attitude to Columba when the saint threw open the doors of the Pictish fortress which had been barred against him, apparently simply by making the sign of the Cross on them: 'Ever after from that day, so long as he lived, the king held this holy and reverend man in very great honour.'[4]

As well as pointing to the ambivalent and complex nature of the relationship between Christianity and paganism, these miracle stories also raise the question of how far Columba's early followers and biographers sought to portray him not just as a Christian saint but also as a hero and strong man in the tradition of the Celtic warrior aristocracy. This is a much-debated topic. In their collection of poems from Iona, Thomas Clancy and Gilbert Márkus show the extent to which the *Amra Choluimb Chille*, the eulogy commissioned very shortly after Columba's death by Aed mac Ainmirech, king of the Cenél Conaill, draws on the language used for pre-Christian Celtic heroes.[5] Other scholars are more cautious about seeing pre-Christian strands in the Irish cult of sainthood and feel that it marks a radical departure from the old tradition of celebrating the heroic lives of chieftains and warlords. Columba himself, of course, had both the old and the new types of heroism in his make-up. The blood of generations of warlords in his Cenél Connaill ancestry mingled with the self-sacrificing asceticism and humility of one who followed Jesus of Nazareth. It would be surprising if his own sainthood, as it came to be asserted and celebrated by his disciples and successors, did not contain something of both these elements.

One aspect of Columba's supernatural power that can be seen either as wholly and exclusively Christian or alternatively as embracing substantial elements from primal Celtic mythology is his frequent encounters with angels and other non-physical beings. The pre-Christian Celts inhabited a world populated by spirits, fairies and demons which often took on physical shape and appeared to mortals. Second sight is a recognised feature of the Celtic character and one would expect Christianity in Celtic lands to take on a particular fascination with the supernatural and the otherworldly. Yet we need to be careful before seeing

Adomnán's frequent references to Columba's sightings of both demons and angels as indicating the survival of an essentially pre-Christian world picture. Early Christians also lived in constant contact with supernatural beings, as of course did the writers of the books that make up the Old and New Testaments. When Adomnán wrote of Columba seeing 'holy angels contending in the air against the hostile powers' and 'a very black host of demons fighting against him with iron darts', he was echoing the language of the Book of Revelation.[6] In seeing the souls of the righteous physically being carried by angels to heaven, Columba himself was similarly sharing the same vision that had animated St Luke's account of the death of Lazarus.

Adomnán describes Columba experiencing at least eighteen encounters with angels. Perhaps the most dramatic is the one reported by a fellow monk who saw angels clad in white robes flying down with great speed and standing around the saint as he stood on a little knoll on Iona praying with his arms spread towards heaven (Book 3, Chapter 17). The presumed site of this encounter, a little hill just off the road down to the machair on the west side of the island, has long been called *Cnoc nan Aingeal*, or the Hill of the Angels. Adomnán also writes more than once of Columba being bathed in heavenly light. During one period of three days and nights when he experienced visitations and spiritual insights on Hinba, the hut in which he resided was filled with light which could be seen escaping from under the doors and through the keyholes while inside Columba could be heard singing spiritual songs of a kind never heard before (Book 3, Chapter 19). On another occasion, St Brendan, attending Mass on the island of Hinba, saw 'a ball of fire like a comet burning very brightly on the head of Columba while he was standing before the altar and consecrating the sacred oblation, and thus it continued burning and rising upwards like a column, so long as he continued to be engaged in the same most sacred mysteries.'[7] Once again, this kind of picture is not without biblical precedent and we are reminded how richly and vividly early Christians followed the writers of the Old and New Testaments in imagining their faith. Whether out of Celtic feyness or Christian conviction, Columba does seem to have had a decidedly mystical bent. Speaking to some of his brethren on Iona about his gift for prophecy, he revealed that 'by some divine intuition and through a wonderful expansion of his inner soul, he beheld the whole universe drawn together and laid open to his sight, as in one ray of sun'.[8]

Some of his miraculous powers were deployed both to encourage his Christian followers and to terrify his pagan opponents. This was particularly true of his apparently superhuman qualities of voice projection, as described by Adomnán:

> *The venerable man, when singing in the church with the brethren, raised his voice so wonderfully that it was sometimes heard four furlongs off, that is five hundred paces, and sometimes eight furlongs, that is one thousand paces. But what is stranger still: to those who were with him in the church, his voice did not seem louder than that of others; and yet at the same time persons more than a mile away heard it so distinctly that they could mark each syllable of the verses he was singing, for his voice sounded the same whether far or near.*

> *Another story concerning the great and wonderful power of his voice should not be omitted. The fact is said to have taken place near the fortress of King Brude (near Inverness). When the saint himself was chanting the evening hymns with a few of the brethren, as usual, outside the king's fortifications, some Druids, coming near to them, did all they could to prevent God's praises being sung in the midst of a pagan nation.*

> *On seeing this, the saint began to sing the 44th Psalm, and
> at the same moment so wonderfully loud, like pealing
> thunder, did his voice become, that king and people were
> struck with terror and amazement.*[9]

John Purser, the distinguished Scottish musicologist, has suggested that Columba may well have mastered the technique of
emphasising harmonics to give the impression that he had two
voices, one sounding the harmonic an octave below the sung note
and emitting a lion-like growl that might well frighten those who
had not heard it before, and the other sounding as though it ema-
nated from somewhere far above the singer's head.[10] It may just
be, of course, that Columba was an exceptionally loud and
enthusiastic singer.

These pictures of Columba chanting psalms, either in church
with his brethren or alone in his retreat on Hinba, take us to the
heart of his life as a monk. The daily office on Iona revolved
around the singing of psalms. Columba's own deep attachment to
the psalms is attested by numerous stories and sources. According
to one tradition it was his childhood habit of visiting the little
church of Tulach Dubhglaise, close to his birthplace, to read the
psalms that led local children to nickname him *Colum Cille* (dove
of the church). The *Irish Life* records that when his tutor, Cruithnechan, forgot the words of Psalm 100 while officiating at a
Christmas Mass, the young Columba, who had only just learned
to read, immediately stepped in and recited the psalm without a
single mistake. Then there is the story that the offence for which
he was punished at the Synod of Teltown and perhaps banished
from Ireland was the illegal copying of a particularly fine psalter
belonging to Finian of Moville. We know from Adomnán's *Life* and
the early eulogistic poems that Columba spent many hours in his
cell copying the psalms. One of the psalters which he produced

may even still exist today in the form of the *Cathach* that bears his name and is preserved in the Royal Irish Academy in Dublin. Among the earliest extant examples of Irish Latin script, this badly damaged and incomplete psalter, which follows the text of St Jerome's translation, has been reliably dated to either the late sixth or early seventh century so it is by no means impossible that it was the work of Columba himself. If that was the case, he was proficient in the art of manuscript illumination. The capital letters at the beginning of each psalm are decorated with spirals, stemmed crosses and the occasional fish or animal head.[11]

The most powerful testimony to Columba's devotion to the psalms is to be found in the *Irish Life's* description of his nightly routine on Iona. He is portrayed as sleeping for just a brief time on the bare earth floor of his cell with a stone for his pillow. Rising, he first cried a lament, 'like a fond mother bewailing her only son', and then went down to the seashore where he chanted all 150 psalms ('the three fifties') before sunrise each morning:

> *The three fifties – sore the watching – in the night;*
> *great was the pain.*
> *In the sea beside Scotland before the sun had risen*
> *Clearly he laid himself in the sand, it was great labour,*
> *The trace of his ribs through his raiment was visible when*
> *the wind blew.*[12]

It is worth noting in passing that Columba is by no means the only Celtic saint who is said to have chanted psalms either in or beside the sea. Bede describes St Cuthbert wading into the waves off Lindisfarne for the same purpose and adds that a pair of otters would sometimes greet him after his long vigil and lick his feet to warm them. One of the reasons why St David acquired the nickname *Aquaticus* is said to have been because he also was prone to stand up to his waist in the sea off Pembrokeshire and chant the psalms in time with the breaking waves. This description of Columba's nightly vigil conveys an impression of extreme asceticism and self-denial. More than any other source, the medieval *Irish Life* emphasises the simplicity and humility of his monastic life. It portrays him taking off the sandals of his fellow monks so that he could wash their feet and bringing their share of corn from the fields on his own back before grinding it himself in the island mill. After describing the chanting of psalms, as above, as his 'nightwork', it gives this account of his regular daytime schedule: 'he attended to the canonical hours; he offered Christ's Body and his Blood; he preached His gospel; he baptised; he consecrated; he anointed; he healed lepers and the blind and lame and folk of every disease besides.'[13]

Monk, priest, preacher, pastor and healer – Columba seems to have fulfilled all of these roles as abbot of Iona. Central to his day was the performance of the monastic offices, celebrated together with other monks in the community's simple wooden church, and the times of private prayer undertaken alone in his cell on Iona and on the remote island of Hinba to which he seems often to have retreated for a period of solitary vigil and fasting. He regularly seems to have presided over celebrations of the Eucharist and to have preached both on Iona and during his travels on the mainland. Adomnán recounts several instances of his baptism of Christian converts and records healing miracles performed through prayer, the laying on of hands and sprinkling with water that he had blessed. He also provides telling examples of the saint's deep pastoral skills, notably in the story of the wife who comes to him because she can no longer face sleeping with her ugly husband. She hopes that Columba will tell her to cross the sea and join a nunnery but in fact he gets her and her husband to fast with him for a day. As they sleep the following evening, he prays for them and the next day the woman awakes transformed – 'That man whom I hated yesterday, I love today; for my heart hath been changed last night in some unknown way from hatred to love.'[14]

Several stories speak in similar terms of Columba's abilities to reconcile people both to themselves and to others from whom they have become distant or estranged. This pastoral gift is often portrayed as being exercised through the medium of penance. Many of those who visited Iona came as penitents, seeking to atone for some crime or to come to terms with feelings of guilt and remorse. Columba seems to have established a special community for penitents at Mag Luinge on Tiree. A story told by Adomnán (Book 2, Chapter 39) shows the extent to which he used both penance and counselling as part of a pastoral ministry founded on the principles of reconciliation and justice. It concerns an Irishman who had killed a man in his native Connaught and had made the long journey to Iona to 'wipe out his sins on a pilgrimage'. Columba told him that he must spend seven years on Tiree. At the end of that period, he returned to the saint to be told that he must now return to the relative who had paid his ransom and saved him from paying the penalty of death. He had promised this man he would serve him for life but had run away. Columba even gave the penitent a decorated sword to give to the deserted master as a peace offering and told him to discharge his debt to his estranged family. This was done and the penitent returned to Iona, took his monastic vows and served for many years as a monk at Mag Luinge where he worked gathering reeds.

Columba was active as a teacher and scholar as well as a priest and pastor. On at least one occasion Adomnán refers to him instructing a pupil in wisdom and divine learning (Book 3, Chapter 20). The monastic school at Iona was to become highly celebrated in the seventh century. I have already alluded to the frequency with which Columba is portrayed, as he is on the front cover of this book, copying the psalms at a desk in his cell. This work seems to have extended to other parts of the Scriptures, notably the Gospels, and may well have spread beyond simple copying of the text to biblical scholarship and analysis. Adomnán comments on Columba's ability to interpret 'the sacred books' in the context of his more general prophetic powers (Book 3, Chapter 18) and Dallán Forgaill's *Amra Choluimb Chille* mentions that he learned Greek grammar in order to aid his biblical studies. This earliest of all the sources on his life in fact portrays Columba as 'learning's pillar in every stronghold' with intellectual interests stretching beyond biblical exegesis and theology into the realms of mathematics and astronomy:

> *He fixed the Psalms,*
> *he made known the books of Law,*
> *those books Cassian loved ...*
> *The books of Solomon, he followed them.*
> *Seasons and calculations he set in motion.*
> *He separated the elements according to figures*
> *among the books of the Law.*
> *He read mysteries*
> *and distributed the Scriptures among the schools,*
> *and he put together the harmony concerning*
> *the course of the moon,*
> *the course which it ran with the rayed sun,*
> *and the course of the sea.*[15]

As the two most recent translators and editors of the *Amra* comment, it is interesting that 'this earliest specimen from Columba's dossier emphasises not his miraculous powers ... but his learning. Dallán's Columba is above all a scholar's saint.'[16]

Did Columba write himself as well as studying the works of

others? A host of poems have been attributed to him, many of them on very dubious grounds. There is, however, good reason for thinking that he did write devotional verses, some of which may have come down to us to provide a first-hand flavour of his mind and his faith. Various pieces of evidence suggest that Columba may have been a poet. There is a tradition that Gemmán, mentioned by Adomnán as Columba's teacher while he was a deacon at Leinster, was a bard who inspired his young charge with a love of the rich body of pre-Christian Irish verse. Adomnán also refers to a 'book of the week's hymns written out by St Columba with his own hand'. It is not clear from this reference, which suggests that the Iona monks had their own weekly cycle of hymns in addition to the psalms, whether Columba was the book's author or simply its copier. A line in the *Amra* – 'He went with two songs to heaven after his cross' – has generally been taken to refer to hymns written by the saint although it could simply indicate that he pursued his love of singing to the very end of his life.[17]

The leading contenders for the Columban hymns mentioned in the *Amra*, if such they be, are probably two Latin poems which begin respectively *Altus Prosator* and *Adiutor Laborantium*. Two other poems, *In Te, Christe*, and *Noli Pater*, also have long-standing traditions of attribution to Columba. It is worth considering both the themes and the circumstances apparently surrounding the composition of these four poems.

Of the numerous poems that have been attributed to Columba over the years, scholars are generally agreed that *Altus Prosator* is the most likely to have been written by him. James Kenney, who made an exhaustive survey of the sources for the early ecclesiastical history of Ireland, believes that we may 'with reasonable probability, regard the *Altus* as a genuine production of the saint of Iona'.[18] The poem has an 'abecedarian' shape with the first word of each verse beginning with a successive letter of the alphabet

from A through to Z, although excluding U and W, making a total
of 23 six-line stanzas. Strongly focused on the person of God the
Father, it centres on the themes of creation, fall and judgement. It
begins with a majestic evocation of the eternal and primordial
nature of God and a clear exposition of the orthodox Christian
theology of the Trinity:

> *The High Creator, Ancient of Days and Unbegotten*
> *was without origin of beginning and without end;*
> *He is and shall be to infinite ages of ages*
> *with Whom is Christ the only begotten*
> *and the Holy Spirit,*
> *coeternal in the everlasting glory of the Godhead.*
> *We set forth not three gods,*
> *but we say there is One God,*
> *saving our faith in three most glorious persons.*[19]

The hymn goes on to catalogue the physical wonders of creation
in verses full of cosmological and astronomical imagery, perhaps
reflecting Columba's strong interest in these themes as reported
in the *Amra*:

> *By the divine powers of the great God is suspended*
> *the globe of earth, and thereto is set the circle*
> *of the great deep*
> *supported by the strong hand of God Almighty,*
> *promontories and rocks sustaining the same,*
> *with columns like bars on solid foundations*
> *immoveable like so many strengthened bases.*[20]

The fall of creation is next graphically described with one stanza
given over to a lurid portrayal of hell. The hymn is pervaded by a

sense of impending judgement – it has been compared to the later *Dies Irae* – and it portrays Christ not so much as the world's redeemer but rather as its judge, at whose descent from heaven 'the stars will fall to the earth as the fruit from a fig tree'. The emphasis throughout the *Altus Prosator* is on the sovereignty and judgement of God. Its overall mood is dark and somewhat frightening. Indeed, with its concentration on the fall and on judgement it seems more Calvinist than Celtic, at least in the sense in which the latter term has been used in recent times.

The preface to the hymn which appears in the Irish *Liber Hymnorum* – an eleventh-century manuscript that cannot be taken as wholly reliable – gives two different versions of how Columba came to compose it. One is that it was written as a penitential exercise when he was troubled by the memory of three battles in which he had played a part, Cúl Drebene in 561, Coleraine in 579, and Cúl Feda near Clonard in 587. The other tradition recorded in the *Liber Hymnorum* and in several other early manuscripts is that the words of *Altus Prosator* came to Columba as he was grinding oats at the mill on Iona in order to make bread for visitors to the monastery. The particular rhythm of the poem, with eight syllables to each line, is said to have been suggested to him by the motion of the quern, or rotary hand mill, that he was using.

The preface to *Altus Prosator* in some manuscripts of the *Liber Hymnorum* gives the additional information that the visitors for whom Columba was making oat-bread were emissaries from Gregory the Great, who was pope from 590 to 604. They had come to Iona bearing presents of a cross and a hymnary. In return, Columba gave them his newly written hymn to take back to Rome. When the hymn was later read out to Pope Gregory, he expressed his view that there was no fault with it 'except the scantiness in it of the praise of the Trinity'.[21] This criticism reached the ears of Columba who responded by writing another hymn, *In Te, Christe,* with a more Trinitarian and Christological focus.

Whatever its provenance, and the above story is almost certainly apocryphal, *In Te, Christe* has probably become the best known to modern Christians of all the poems supposedly written by Columba. Translated by Duncan MacGregor for the thirteen hundredth anniversary of Columba's death in 1897, it appears in many hymnals, generally set to the ancient Irish tune *Moville*, and begins:

> *Christ is the world's redeemer,*
> *the lover of the pure,*
> *the fount of heavenly wisdom,*
> *our trust and hope secure,*
> *the armour of his soldiers,*
> *the lord of earth and sky,*
> *our health while we are living,*
> *our life when we shall die.*

Another quite likely Columban composition is the short hymn *Adiutor Laborantium*. It shares with *Altus Prosator* an abecederian structure. Discovered in an eleventh century manuscript of devotional and liturgical material from Winchester, it is mentioned in the *Liber Hymnorum* as having been composed just before the *Altus Prosator* when Columba was walking from the refectory to the mill on Iona with the sack of oats on his back. This may explain the first line of what is in effect a litany of God's attributes, 'O helper of workers'. The hymn dramatically changes mood half way through and becomes a much more personal cry for help:

> *I beg that me, a little man*
> *trembling and most wretched,*
> *rowing through the infinite storm*
> *of this age,*

> Christ may draw after Him to the lofty
> most beautiful haven of life.[22]

This graphic metaphor of the individual human 'rowing through the infinite storm' surely comes from the pen, if not of Columba himself, then of one of his fellow brothers on Iona. Facing regular journeys across the sea surrounding their island base with its treacherous currents and whirlpools, they must have been all too aware of the fragility and vulnerability of human life. Adomnán recounts several instances of storms suddenly blowing up, and the *Irish Annals* record the wrecking of several boats carrying members of the community to and from Iona with serious loss of life. In 691, for example, six monks were reported to have drowned when their boat was overturned in a severe gale.

The fourth poem attributed to Columba in early Irish manuscript sources is also a cry for God's protection against disaster. *Noli Pater* begins with a plea to God not to allow thunder and lightning 'lest we be shattered by its fear and its fire'. One of the manuscripts of the *Liber Hymnorum* suggests that Columba composed it when an oak wood had been set alight by a bolt of lightning. Another version, which also mentions lightning setting fire to a wood, relates that he offered up the short hymn, which continues by expressing both fear and praise of God, while standing at the door of a hermitage in Derry. Its association with an oak wood carries echoes of pre-Christian Celtic religion where oak groves were particularly sacred and provided the location for the sacrificial rituals carried out by Druids, and there is something of the feel of a charm or incantation about the hymn. According to the preface in the *Liber Hymnorum* 'whoever recites it at lying down and rising up, it protects him against lightning flash, and it protects the nine persons of his household whom he chooses.'[23] A more Christian gloss on the poem in another manuscript suggests that it is, in fact, an allegory on the theme of the Last Judgement. Whatever its purpose and provenance, it ends with a delightful and vivid image:

*The flame of God's love dwells in my heart
as a jewel of gold is placed in a silver dish.*[24]

These poems reflect many of the themes which ran through Columba's life, as portrayed by Adomnán. His is an idealised portrait, the work of a hagiographer rather than a biographer, but even granted this, it is impossible not to read it without sensing the sanctity of someone who combined courage, mysticism, poetic and pastoral gifts and austerity in unusual measure:

From his boyhood he had been brought up in Christian training in the study of wisdom, and by the grace of God had so preserved the integrity of his body, and the purity of soul, that though dwelling on earth he appeared to live like the saints in heaven. For he was angelic in appearance, graceful in speech, holy in work, with talents of the highest order, and consummate prudence; he lived a soldier of Christ during thirty-four years in an island. He never could spend the space of even one hour without study, or prayer, or writing, or some other holy occupation. So incessantly was he engaged night and day in the unwearied exercise of fasting and watching, that the burden of each of these austerities would seem beyond the power of all human endurance.[25]

The most moving part of Adomnán's *Life* is his account of Columba's last days on Iona. It is difficult to do justice to this passage without reproducing it in full and those readers who do not know it are urged to have recourse to one of the excellent modern translations and savour it for themselves. Suffice it to say that in his last hours on earth Columba is portrayed as engaging in many of the activities that have characterised his lifelong ministry. He goes round the island in a cart visiting the brothers at work in the fields and telling them of his forthcoming death. He attends Sunday mass and has a vision of 'an angel of the Lord flying above actually inside the house of prayer'. He blesses the heaps of grain stored in the barn ready for the community's use through the winter. Then, after his poignant encounter with the old horse which used to carry the milk-pails and now puts its head against his bosom and weeps, he climbs the little hill overlooking the monastery and blesses the island, prophesying that it will come to be reverenced by Christians and non-Christians far round the world. Returning to his hut, he sits copying out the psalms, stopping when he reaches the tenth verse of Psalm 34: 'Those that seek the Lord shall not want for anything that is good.' He then goes to vespers and returns to sleep on the bare rock floor of his hut with a stone for his pillow. After briefly resting, he summons the brethren, telling them:

> *These, O my children, are the last words I address to you – that ye be at peace and have unfeigned charity among yourselves; and if you thus follow the example of the holy fathers, God, the Comforter of the good, will be your Helper, and I, abiding with Him, will intercede for you; and He will not only give you sufficient to supply the wants of this present life, but will also bestow on you the good and eternal rewards which are laid up for those that keep His commandments.*[26]

As the bell rings out for the midnight office, Columba runs ahead of the other monks into church and kneels alone in prayer before the altar. At that moment the whole church is filled with angelic light around the saint. Helped by his faithful servant Diarmait, he raises his right arm to bless the choir of monks and at that moment the venerable abbot gives up the ghost, his face transfixed with a wonderful joy and gladness 'no doubt seeing the holy angels coming to meet him'.[27]

Columba's passing from this world, like his arrival into it, was accompanied by signs and wonders, miracles and angelic apparitions. In death his powers of prophecy, pastoral aid and protection were to be undiminished. Indeed, his stature as a saint grew steadily as his posthumous cult spread far beyond the bounds of the tiny island on which he had chosen to spend the last thirty five years of his life.

I cannot resist ending this chapter by quoting in full one other poem traditionally attributed to Columba even though it was almost certainly written by someone else. It has him yearning to be back on a headland in northern Ireland, the Uchd Ailiun of the first line, and brings together his love of the natural world, especially the sea and all contained within it, his thirst for learning, his pastoral heart, his strong sense of penitence and contrition and his deep faith.

> *Delightful would it be to me to be in Uchd Ailiun*
> *On the pinnacle of a rock,*
> *That I might often see*
> *The face of the ocean;*
> *That I might see its heaving waves*
> *Over the wide ocean,*
> *When they chant music to their Father*
> *Upon the world's course;*
> *That I might see its level sparkling strand,*
> *It would be no cause of sorrow;*
> *That I might hear the song of the wonderful birds,*
> *Source of happiness;*

That I might hear the thunder of the crowding waves
    Upon the rocks;
That I might hear the roar by the side of the church
    Of the surrounding sea;
That I might see its noble flocks
    Over the watery ocean;
That I might see the sea monsters,
    The greatest of all wonders;
That I might see its ebb and flood
    In their career;
That my mystical name might be, I say,
    Cul ri Erin [Back turned to Ireland];
That contrition might come upon my heart
    Upon looking at her;
That I might bewail my evils all,
    Though it were difficult to compute them;
That I might bless the Lord
    Who orders all;
Heaven with its countless bright orders,
    Land, strand and flood,
That I might search in all the books
    That would help my soul;
At times kneeling to the Heaven of my heart,
    At times singing psalms;
At times contemplating the King of Heaven,
    Chief of the Holy Ones;
At times at work without compulsion,
    This would be delightful.
At times plucking duilisc from the rocks
    At other times fishing
At times distributing food to the poor
    At times in a hermitage.[28]

Notes

1   George Campbell, 8th Duke of Argyll, *Iona* (Strahan & Co., London, 1870), pp.42 & 43
2   Thomas Owen Clancy and Gilbert Márkus, *IONA*, p.116
3   *Life of St Columba*, written by Adamnán and translated by William Reeves (Edmonston & Douglas, Edinburgh, 1874) p.56
4   *Life of Columba*, p.62
5   *IONA*, pp.123-24
6   *Life of Columba*, pp. 82 & 83. Compare Revelation 12.7
7   *Life of Columba*, p.90
8   *Life of Columba*, pp.6-7
9   *Life of Columba*, p.28
10 John Purser, *Scotland's Music* (Mainstream Publishing, Edinburgh 1992), pp.33-34
11 For more information on the Cathach, see the website: https://www.ria.ie/cathach-psalter-st-columba
12 *Betha Choluim Chille: On the Life of St Columba* trans. Whitley Stokes (Calcutta, 1877), p.123
13 *Betha Choluim Chille*, p.125
14 *Life of Columba*, p.71
15 *IONA*, pp.107-9
16 *IONA*, p.122
17 *IONA*, p.111
18 James Kenney, *The Sources for the Early History of Ireland: Ecclesiastical* (Padraic ÓTailliur, Dublin, 1979), p.263
19 *The Irish Liber Hymnorum* edited by J.H. Bernard and R. Atkinson (Henry Bradshaw Society, London, 1898), vol.II, p.150
20 *Liber Hymnorum*, Vol.II, p.152
21 *Liber Hymnorum*, Vol.II, p.25
22 *IONA*, p.73
23 *Liber Hymnorum*, V ol. II, p.28
24 *IONA*, p.85
25 *Life of Columba*, p.3

26   *Life of Columba, p.97*

27   *Life of Columba, p.98*

28   *Lyra Celtica* edited by Elizabeth Sharp (Patrick Geddes, Edinburgh, 1896), pp.20-21

Four

The character
of the Columban church

Did Columba introduce or exemplify a new and distinctive form of Christian doctrine and practice? Can we, indeed, speak of Columban Christianity in the same way that we can talk about Lutheranism, Methodism or Benedictine monasticism?

To begin to answer these questions we need to strip away more layers of myth-making. In the centuries since his death Columba has been hailed by apologists from many different denominational and theological standpoints as the precursor or founding father of their particular brand of faith. Scottish Presbyterians, Episcopalians and Roman Catholics have perhaps been the most assiduous claimants to the Columban heritage, each maintaining that the church which he planted on Iona anticipated in some important respect their own distinctive denominational characteristics. This anachronistic and partisan use of history was roundly and rightly condemned more than a century ago by the eighth Duke of Argyll. Noting that the distinctive features of the monastic system introduced by Columba on Iona 'have much exercised the ingenuity of Presbyterian and Episcopalian controversialists', he pointed to the futility of looking 'in the peculiarities of the Scoto-Irish Church for the model either of primitive practice or of any modern system. As regards the theology of Columba's time, although it was not what we now understand as Roman, neither assuredly was it what we understand as Protestant.'[1]

The fact is that, unlike Martin Luther, John Calvin or John Wesley, Columba was neither the instigator of a new movement in the history of Christianity nor the founder of a new church. Indeed, he himself would have had no sense of belonging to a distinct denomination as most Christians do today. He belonged to an age where the church was thought of in universal terms rather than as a series of national or confessional bodies. Columba owed his allegiance first and foremost to Jesus Christ. He had a strong sense of the universality of the family which made up the members of His body on earth. This is not to say that he did not have other more particular and personal loyalties as well. As we have already seen, he retained strong ties of kinship with the Uí Néill princes in northern Ireland. He doubtless thought of himself as Irish and identified with fellow Irish settlers (*Scoti*) in Dál Riata. This particular sense of ethnic and cultural identity may have been intensified by the difficulty in communicating with other peoples living in what is now Scotland, most notably the Picts, in conversing with whom he needed an interpreter. Writing about the monks of Iona, including Columba, Donald Meek has sensibly if tentatively suggested that 'they might have regarded themselves as Irish or Gaelic, if indeed they had any rudimentary notion of these matters. More probably, they would have defined themselves over and against the Picts and the Britons with whom they came into contact'.[2]

Columba would most certainly not have seen himself belonging to the kind of distinct Celtic church so often associated with him by historians and Christians of a romantic persuasion. The notion of a Celtic church, conceived of as a distinct ecclesiastical entity clearly distinguishable from, if not actually in opposition to, the Roman church, is profoundly misleading. It presupposes a degree of uniformity among the highly diverse Celtic tribes and peoples of Europe and a sense of self-conscious separatism which simply did not exist. The modern revival of interest in so-called 'Celtic Christianity' has unfortunately perpetuated and encouraged the myth of the Celtic church. We need to heed the sober and salutary words of the distinguished medieval historian Professor Wendy Davies: 'There was no such thing as a Celtic church: the concept is unhelpful, if not positively harmful.'[3]

This does not mean that there was nothing to distinguish the Christian beliefs and practices of the Irish-born and educated Columba from those of his near-contemporary, St Augustine of

Canterbury, whose theological education and monastic experience had been in Rome. The invention by over-zealous Protestants and nationalists of a wholly spurious Celtic church standing over and against the Roman Church has had more than one distorting effect. As well as greatly over-exaggerating the extent of distinct and self-conscious Celtic separatism, it has also provoked a counter-reaction which has equally overstated the Roman influence on all early medieval Christian communities, including those in the British Isles. An example of this is Professor Jocelyn Toynbee's statement that 'the so-called Celtic church, surviving continuously in the west and north, was thoroughly Roman in Creed and origins; Roman too, initially in its organisation and practice'.[4] It is true that the theology of Columba, based as it was on the Scriptures, the writings of the Latin and Greek Fathers and the historic creeds of the church, would have struck Augustine as essentially orthodox and that he would have found much that was familiar in the Latin liturgy used on Iona with its close affinity to the Roman ordinary of the Mass. In other areas, however, there were some differences between both the outlook and the practices prevailing in Canterbury and Iona – most notably in ecclesiastical organisation and monastic lifestyle.

The numerous Christian communities which were in existence throughout Europe, North Africa and the Eastern Mediterranean by the sixth century AD exhibited a rich diversity of local cultural, social, intellectual and liturgical influences and practices. The Christian church may have been conceived of in more universal, international and non-denominational terms than it is now but it was not monolithic in its structures and ethos. Geographical and linguistic factors undoubtedly played a part in bringing certain communities together and forging particular spheres of common influence and practice. These were not always as one might expect – Iona, in common with other monastic communities on the

western side of the British Isles, had at least as much contact with
Egyptian and Syrian Christianity as with Rome. There were
elements of xenophobic chauvinism at work as well. A seventh-
century Irish abbot was said to have held that 'Rome is wrong.
Jerusalem is wrong. Antioch is wrong. Only the *Scoti* and Britons
know what is right'. Given their close geographical proximity, it
was not surprising that Christian communities formed by the
Irish, the British and the Picts should display certain affinities as
well as have their own distinct local characteristics. Increasingly,
anthropologists and historians of religion stress the theme of
inculturation, the extent to which all faiths, including Christianity,
adapt themselves to and are shaped by the particular cultures in
which they take root. As Thomas Clancy and Gilbert Márkus
point out, to dismiss such phrases as Celtic Christianity and the
Celtic church is not to rule out any connection between the local
cultures of the Celtic peoples and the way they practised Christianity. 'It is only to deny that it was the same "Celtic" way among
all these peoples. Christianity had its local, particular aspects in
early Ireland and Britain, but its aspects were many and varied
from region to region and from people to people.'[5]

This chapter, and indeed this book as a whole, is dealing with
one of these particular strands, or 'inculturations' of Christianity
in Celtic Britain. We are, I think, justified in calling it Columban
Christianity or perhaps more accurately the Columban church.
Columba, as we have already noted, was a church-planter. If he
did not found a new denomination or a new movement, he mani-
festly did found monasteries, most notably on Iona and also elsewhere in Scots Dál Riata and in Ireland. These monasteries formed
a definite *paruchia* or family, which came to have its own common
rule, at least in the century following Columba's death if not
during his lifetime. The Columban *familia*, which grew consider-
ably in both size and importance through the seventh and eighth

centuries, looked for leadership to successive abbots of Iona in the highly personalised form of authority and organisation which had been established by the founder. Sally Foster has rightly observed that 'the term "Columban church" is not without drawbacks since it plays down the unsung role of less well-documented saints' but it is preferable to 'the Celtic church' and provided we use it carefully to describe the particular characteristics of the Christian community which flourished on Iona and its wider *paruchia* from the mid-sixth to the mid-ninth centuries, it can, I think, be positively helpful and fruitful.[6]

The single most striking and important feature of the Columban church was its monastic character. In this, of course, it corresponded to earlier Irish foundations associated with such figures as Finnian of Clonard, Finnian of Moville and Ciarán of Clonmacnoise, although not with the church established by St Patrick in the mid-fifth century. The extent to which Patrick deliberately sought to provide Ireland with an episcopally administered church organised on a diocesan system with parish churches as the key units of local mission is a matter of some debate. What is not in dispute is that within a generation or so of his death the dominant institution of Irish Christianity had become the monastery, with the parish church being eclipsed in importance and the authority of diocesan bishops being effectively taken over by abbots. Columba was, of course, the supreme exemplar of an abbot who wielded far more power and influence than a bishop, a matter which Bede found particularly worthy of note. However he always seems to have deferred to the authority of a visiting bishop in liturgical matters and allowed him to celebrate the Eucharist.

The apparent subordination of bishops to abbots in the Columban church has long been made much of by Presbyterians and others seeking historical precedents for non-episcopal forms of ecclesiastical government. In fact, it is unlikely to have rested on any high-minded theories of democracy or power-sharing based on biblical principles. Monasteries took root in Ireland because they suited the social and geographical configuration of the country. Parish churches and dioceses worked well in more centralised and urbanised societies but were not appropriate for remote rural communities. The structure of the monastic *familia* paralleled that of the *túaths*, the small kingships into which Ireland was divided. It was not surprising that in a society based on ties of kinship and family, abbots should come to take on something of the status of kings, especially since many, like those of Iona, held their office through hereditary succession. Monastic *paruchiae* formed tribes which coexisted alongside their secular equivalents. As well as becoming the spiritual centres of the *túaths*, monasteries adopted some of the physical characteristics of the hill-forts and strongholds of their rulers, being protected by a *vallum*, or boundary bank and ditch, and a wooden stockade which surrounded a small township of dwelling huts, workshops and communal buildings.

It was this Irish model of being the church that Columba brought to Scotland when he planted his community on Iona in or around 563. In the words of the Scottish historian Archie Duncan, 'What Columba brought was not a Gospel hitherto unheard, but a way of religious life in eremitical communities following the rule of the founder abbot and seeking spiritual maturity through work and meditation.'[7] Behind its immediate Irish antecedents lay deeper roots which gave the monastic life of Iona and of the Columban church as a whole much of its special character. The origins of Christian monasticism lie in fourth-century Egypt and Syria where the desert fathers felt the call to withdraw from the world and either retreated into solitary cells or established corporate communities living according to a strict rule of life. The pioneer of the eremitical or solitary life is often taken to be St Antony of Egypt and the development of cenobitic or common-life monasticism is particularly associated with Pachomius. Introduced to western Europe through the writings of Athanasius and John Cassian, and the example of Martin of Tours who founded his own monastery at Ligugé in Gaul in 361, the ideas and practices of the desert fathers profoundly influenced Columba and his successors. References in early poems written by monks associated with Iona suggest that Athanasius' *Life of St Antony*, Sulpicius Severus' *Life of Martin of Tours* and Cassian's *Conferences*, which give an account of the teaching and practices of the early Egyptian monks and hermits, were among the most thumbed volumes in the island's library.

Several pieces of evidence point to trading contact between the eastern Mediterranean and Iona. Archaeological digs on the island have uncovered pieces of red pottery from Carthage in North Africa and fragments of amphorae, containers for olive oil and wine, thought to come from Asia Minor. Some of the pigments used for colouring illuminated manuscripts can only have been imported from the Near East and the little red dots which fringe the capital letters on the psalter traditionally associated with Columba and known as his *Cathach* seem to be inspired by decorative work found on Coptic manuscripts in Egyptian monasteries. It has even been suggested that the rectangular layout of the monastic settlement on Iona was based on an Egyptian or Syrian design. While one or two other Irish foundations were surrounded by a similar rectangular *vallum*, most notably Clonmacnoise, the great majority of both Irish and Scottish monastic compounds were circular in shape.

It is impossible to gain any impression of the scale or the appearance of the original monastery on Iona from the restored buildings of the much later Benedictine foundation which form the present abbey. Columba's community had no stone buildings and lived, worked, prayed and slept in a collection of wooden huts and wattle and daub shelters which covered an area possibly extending to twenty acres. Some monks lived alone while others seem to have enjoyed a more communal existence, sleeping in dormitories. At the centre of the compound was a small wooden church and around it the guest house, kitchen and refectory, library and *scriptorium* (where manuscripts were copied and studied), barns for storing grain, a smithy and workshops for working with metal, wood, leather and glass. Beyond the *vallum* were almost five hundred acres of fields on which the community kept cattle and sheep, and grew wheat, oats and other crops. A small fleet of boats was maintained both for fishing and for ferrying monks and visitors to and from the island.

It has been estimated that there may have been around one hundred and fifty monks resident on Iona by the time of Columba's death. They were divided into three main groupings – *seniores*, who were largely responsible for the services in church; working brothers, who seem to have done the bulk of the manual labour in the workshops and fields; and *juniores*, who were novices under instruction. It is not entirely clear if the distinction was made purely in terms of age or if there was a separate category of lay brothers who carried out much of the manual work. In addition to the resident novices, students and pupils came to the island for shorter periods of study. There was also a steady stream of guests and pilgrims passing through Iona, including monks from other communities and penitents seeking to atone for crimes and misdemeanours. Several of the latter were directed on to the remoter communities on Hinba and Tiree where monks from Iona also regularly went on solitary retreat to find their 'place of resurrection'. The general impression is of a busy and bustling community with a very cosmopolitan flavour. Although the original monks on Iona were probably all Irish, they were soon joined by recruits from other parts of the British Isles and possibly from further afield. The first of the community to die was a Briton and Adomnán mentions two Englishmen and a Pict among those monks on the island in Columba's time. Despite its seemingly remote location, and the fact that it could be cut off by bad weather for several days at a time, Iona was not isolated from the outside world. Pointing to the comprehensiveness of its library, Clancy and Márkus comment: 'Here we find a monastery not out on a limb, doing its own "Celtic" thing, but steeped in the culture of Latin Christianity' – and, one might add, Eastern Christianity as well.[8]

It would be wrong to gain an impression of Iona as primarily a transit-camp-cum-tourist-resort. It is true that there was much coming and going and this was why Columba put so much stress on hospitality and told his monks to minister to all their guests, including, as Adomnán's lovely story tells us, the crane which flew in from Ireland. It was the resident community of monks who constituted the heart and soul of the monastery, their lives of self-mortification and daily offering of the sacrifice of praise which provided its raison d'être. In common with the inmates of most Irish monasteries, the monks of Iona followed a lifestyle that was a good deal more strict and austere than that pursued by those in the Continental houses founded by St Benedict and his followers. Indeed, the influence on Irish monasticism of the radical asceticism of the desert fathers of Egypt and Syria provides one indisputable difference between Celtic and Roman Christianity in the early medieval period.

In his classic work on the subject written in 1931, John Ryan listed four main characteristics which made Irish monasticism distinctive. The first was its severe bodily austerity, exemplified in long periods of fasting and vigil, which he saw as deriving directly from Egypt. The leading figures in the monastic movement in

Continental Europe, by contrast, took a more relaxed view and prescribed a less demanding lifestyle in their foundations. The daily rations which each monk was allowed by St Benedict, for example, included a pound of bread, two dishes of cooked food, a dish of fruit or young vegetables and more than half a pint of wine, a menu which, in Ryan's words, 'would have shocked the Fathers of the desert and have sounded incredible to Irish ears'.[9] Benedictine monks were also able to enjoy eight hours of unbroken sleep, a luxury denied to members of the Iona community who were awoken three times during the night for vigils.

The second distinctive feature of Irish monasticism singled out by John Ryan was the combination of eremitical and cenobitic practices within the same communities, with solitary anchorites alongside monks living in community – a testimony, perhaps, to that balanced rhythm of life which we have already noted as a major theme in the Irish monastic tradition. Thirdly, he pointed to a zeal for studying native language and literature as well as biblical and theological literature in Latin and Greek, and lastly he noted the prominence of abbots as ecclesiastical rulers, a development which he felt might partly have arisen 'from an ascetical fear of the worldly advantages then commonly attached to the episcopal office'. Abbots were entrusted with authority because they were felt to be less prone than bishops to worldly temptations and luxurious lifestyles.[10]

All four of these features are to be found in the Columban monastic *familia*. They also figure prominently in the monastic rule which bears the saint's name. First found in Irish in a manuscript in the Burgundian Library in Brussels, the *Rule of Columcille* cannot be traced back beyond the ninth century and it is unlikely that it was actually the work of Columba himself. However, it is reasonable to assume that it embodies principles which had come to be established by his successors as abbots of Iona and it may well reflect the feelings of the founder. The rule, which is striking in its severity and austerity, begins with a commendation of both the eremitic and the cenobitic life and an injunction to 'be always naked in imitation of Christ'. This is followed by a call to develop 'a mind prepared for red martyrdom' (i.e. laying down one's life for the faith) and 'a mind fortified and steadfast for white martyrdom' (the form of witness to Christ particularly dear to the Irish saints which involved dying to self and to all attachments, leaving home and family and going into perpetual exile). Although not as specific as some Irish monastic rules which laid down detailed regulations concerning daily genuflections, vigils and periods of fasting and prayer, the *Rule of Columcille* clearly stipulates a regime of rigorous self-denial:

> *Take not of food till thou art hungry.*
> *Sleep not till thou feelest desire.*
> *Speak not except on business.*[11]

The *Rule of Columcille* prescribes three daily labours: reading, work and prayer. The emphasis on reading reinforces what we have already observed in looking at Columba's own life about the importance of study and scholarship in the community on Iona. Manual work was also regarded as a staple ingredient of the monastic life. The rule divides it into three parts: 'firstly, thine own work, and the work of thy place as regards its real wants; secondly, thy share of the brethren's work; and lastly, to help thy neighbours, viz. by instruction, or writing, or sewing garments or whatever they may be in want of'.[12] The implication here seems to be that all members of the community took part in manual labour, not just the 'working brothers' whose special vocation it was. The third daily work, that of prayer and devotion, occupies the largest part of the rule. The monks are enjoined to 'constant prayers for those who trouble thee' and 'fervour in singing the office of the dead, as if every faithful dead was a particular friend of thine ... Let thy vigils be constant from eve to eve ... Thy measure of prayer shall be until thy tears come; or thy measure of work of labour till thy tears come; or thy measure of thy work of labour or of thy genuflections until thy perspiration often comes, if thy tears are not free.'[13]

What are we to make of this exhortation to tears, not as one might imagine of compassion, but rather of exhaustion? It brings us up against the hard and almost unbearably demanding ethos of Irish monasticism, a world away from the comfortable, easy, attractive spirituality of Celtic Christianity as it is often portrayed today. The constant injunctions to fasting and mortification, genuflection and self-flagellation that fill the gloomy penitentials and stern rules which come out of the early Irish monasteries and their offshoots on mainland Britain may seem unattractive and even bordering on the masochistic to us today. That is because we have lost the sense which our ancestors had of the mysterious power of sacrifice, understood in terms of a reciprocal process of self-offering by God and self-giving by his creatures. Columba and his contemporaries, so close in outlook to and so influenced by the demanding spirituality of the desert fathers, had a deep understanding and appreciation of the intimate if paradoxical connection between self-sacrifice and self-fulfilment, martyrdom and resurrection. We can only begin to enter into their minds as we engage with this dark and somewhat forbidding aspect of their faith.

How then can we best discern and describe the distinctive essence of Columban Christianity, the faith and practice both of the saint himself and of the church which he established on Iona and elsewhere? At the risk of gross over-simplification, and of sounding very sermonic, I propose answering this question by identifying a triple trinity of themes. I employ this device partly because the number three was so important to the Celts, whose pre-Christian religion centred around triads of deities and whose Christianity found one of its most characteristic expressions in a particular devotion to the doctrine of the Trinity. The distinctive characteristics of the Columban church can, I think, be described in terms of a devotional base built on prayer, psalms and poetry, a theology of praise, protection and presence, and an ecclesiology (not a word that Columba and his followers would ever have dreamed of using) of penitence, provisionality and pilgrimage. If you notice a fondness for alliteration here (and for the letter 'p' in particular), you will find even more of it in my book *Following the Celtic Way* (2018) where I identify and explore 21 key beliefs and practices of Celtic Christianity, all beginning with 'p'!

Prayer, undertaken both individually and corporately, was at the heart of the spiritual life of the Columban church. The monks spent long periods praying alone in their cells, often standing with their arms outstretched and raised in what was known as the cross vigil. Several times during the day and night the ringing of a bell summoned them to church to recite the Divine Office. There seem to have been five canonical hours during the day – prime, terce, sext, nones and vespers – while the night office was apparently divided into three separate services – *Ad initium noctis* (at night-fall), *Ad medium noctis* (at midnight) and *Ad matutinam* (very early in the morning towards daybreak). Mass was celebrated on Sundays and feast days at sext, the midday service.

We know relatively little about the forms of worship in the Columban church, although it is clear that they used Latin rather than Irish Gaelic. The main weekly celebration of the eucharist on Iona seems to have taken place in the small church. The Gospel was read outside where lay members, catechumens (those undergoing instruction prior to baptism), penitents and visitors remained while the monks processed into the church with the presiding priest. There are references to services being sung and, as we have already noted, Adomnán mentions a book of weekly hymns which had either been copied out or written by Columba himself. It may well have resembled the *Bangor Antiphonary* which dates from the late seventh century and provides hymns for the Mass and other services. Unfortunately there are no surviving liturgies from Iona. The earliest Irish and Scottish liturgies which are still in existence, the *Stowe Missal* and the *Book of Deer*, both of which probably date from the early ninth century, broadly follow the Roman rite but also show traces of Gallican, Mozarabic (Spanish) and Eastern Mediterranean influence.

If it is impossible to reconstruct the eucharistic liturgy used on Iona during and after Columba's time, we are on much surer ground when it comes to the daily services held at the canonical hours. The Divine Office consisted primarily of the recitation of psalms. It is not quite clear how long it took the monks to get through all one hundred and fifty psalms though there is evidence that in Irish monasteries generally more psalms were chanted at each service, particularly during night vigils, than in either Continental European or Eastern monasteries. Columba's followers and successors seem to have shared his own special attachment to this part of the Scriptures. Chanted, recited, copied, studied and prayed, the psalms were central to the spiritual and devotional life of the Columban church. Their imagery almost certainly influenced its theology. Certainly the three theological themes that I have identified as particularly strong in Columban Christianity – praise, protection and presence – are all very strongly represented in the psalter.

The psalms may well also have been a major influence on the third strand which I have identified in the devotional life of the Columban church – its poetic quality. What I have in mind here is the tendency, shared by many other Celtic Christian communities, to pray in poems rather than in prose and to express faith in images rather than concepts. It is not surprising that those so steeped in the vivid imagery of the psalms should be inclined to express their faith in this way and also to give more prominence in worship to the physical elements and to raw human emotions like anger and despair than other Christian traditions which have put more premium on reasonable moderation and carefully measured prose.

Other factors also contributed to this characteristic of the early British and Irish church. Pre-Christian Celtic society accorded a high role to poets. In Ireland the *filid*, or bards, were a much venerated and respected group who were seen as guardians of the great oral tradition of folklore and heroic legend which sustained the community and provided its roots. Often attached to royal households, the *filid* effectively constituted a distinct order living off public subsidy. The coming of Christianity did not overthrow this reverence for poets and poetry although it brought about an important change in replacing an oral culture with a written one. The monks who toiled away in the monastic *scriptoria* did not simply copy psalters and Gospel books. They also wrote down, for the first time, poems and legends about heroes and battles from the pre-Christian past which had previously been passed down by word of mouth. Zeal for native language and literature was one of the characteristics which John Ryan noted as distinguishing Irish from Continental monasticism. It suggested a broad and inclusive approach affirming traditional poems and songs and integrating them in the new literary-based Christian culture.

There is a very interesting story that first surfaces in an appendix to the *Irish Life* about Columba going to a convention in Druim Ceat in Ireland in 575 partly for the specific purpose of defending poets. There was a move to disband and banish the *filid* because of 'the multitude and the sharpness of their tongues and their complaining and for their evil words. Moreover they had made satires against Aed, King of Ireland.'[14] Columba remonstrated with the king, who was present at the convention, telling him that the praise made by poets 'lasts you eternally' in contrast to transitory eulogies of sycophantic courtiers. Aed relented and, apparently at Columba's suggestion, decreed that rather than being disbanded, the order of *filid* should be reorganised. This portrayal of the saint as a friend of the creative arts seems to square with what we know of the activities undertaken by the monks on Iona which appear to have included manuscript illumination, metalwork, leatherwork and jewellery-making. Columba and his successors clearly valued creative imagination and felt that the arts stood not at the margins of the church but rather at its very centre.

Behind this encouragement of artists and poets lay a belief that story, symbol and metaphor were at least as important in putting across the mysteries of the Christian faith as argument, concept and debate. The Columban church did not produce any great practitioners or texts in the disciplines of philosophical or systematic theology. This is not to say that there was no interest in the big questions with which they deal. Its theology, however, was rooted in its liturgy and devotional life and expressed in hymns of praise like *Altus Prosator* rather than being confined to the schoolroom or the study and formulated in academic treatises. The Columban church, indeed, exemplified the principle of *lex orandi, lex credendi* – it was a worshipping community which believed that God was to be found through prayer and contemplation rather than a debating society which sought to find proofs and arguments for God's existence through rigorous debate and disputation.

Having said that, is it possible to discern a distinctive Columban theology? It has been fashionable to suggest that Celtic Christianity as a whole developed a theology which was more creation-centred and affirmative of the natural world than that of

Rome and of later Catholicism and Protestantism. Something of that does seem to come across in the poem attributed (almost certainly erroneously) to Columba quoted at the end of the last chapter. Yet, one has to say that on the basis of early documents from Iona which have only relatively recently become available in modern English translations and subjected to scholarly analysis, we cannot apply this generalisation to the Columban church. The overwhelming themes of the *Altus Prosator*, as we have seen, are the fall of creation and the judgement of God. Nature is portrayed not in positive 'green' terms but rather as a wild and terrifying power from which humans need to be protected. Nor is there any trace of a Pelagian emphasis on the intrinsic goodness and potential of human nature in these early poems from Iona, some of which may have been the work of Columba himself. Thomas Clancy and Gilbert Márkus point out that both the *Adiutor laborantium* and *Noli pater* are, in fact, deeply Augustinian and anti-Pelagian in their stress on the utter inadequacy of the Christian's own moral strength and their insistence that humans are totally dependent on the grace of God. Indeed, they find this position reflected in many other early Irish texts, leading them to the view that 'there is no support in Irish monastic literature for the claim that there is a uniquely "Celtic" theology of grace which is unlike that of the rest of Latin Christendom'.[15]

If we have to be slightly careful about identifying Columban Christianity as creation-centred, then we certainly need have no qualms about asserting its God-centredness. The two, of course, are not incompatible but it is the latter which comes across particularly strongly in the early literary remains from Iona. Continual praise of God and his wondrous acts is the central raison d'être of a monastic community and it is hardly surprising that the theme of praise, so clearly enjoined in the psalms recited daily by the monks, should bulk so large in the writings of Columba and his successors. The *Altus Prosator* begins as a hymn of praise to the Trinity. As we have already noted, it is rich in cosmological and astronomical detail and to that extent does focus on God's work of creation. Yet although it is lyrical in its evocation of the circling planets and the starry heavens, it makes virtually no reference to the beauties of God's creation on earth. Indeed the theme so often associated with Celtic Christianity of praising God through the beauty of nature is noticeably absent from virtually all the authenticated texts which have come down to us from the Columban church. None of the extant early poems or prayers from Iona exhibits the kind of delight in nature found in the Welsh praise poems, which have been lovingly analysed and identified by Donald Allchin and Oliver Davies, or in the poems and prayers from the (predominantly Outer) Hebrides collected in the late nineteenth century by Alexander Carmichael and published in the *Carmina Gadelica*.[16] In the introduction to the original edition of his collection, Carmichael remarked that 'some of the hymns may have been composed within the cloistered cells of Derry and Iona'.[17] In fact, it is highly unlikely that any of them came from monasteries within the Columban *familia*, which were, of course, without cloisters and where the praise of God seems to have been altogether more heaven-centred.

Reacting against the unhistorical romanticism of some of its modern enthusiasts, several scholars have questioned Celtic Christianity's supposed love affair with nature. Clancy and Márkus, for example, suggest that the lyrical nature poems which they concede are found in some early Irish monastic manuscripts, if not in those from Iona, were the work of cultivated literary teachers and administrators in the large monastic towns – 'the real hermit, living in a damp stone or wooden cell, fasting in hot and cold weather to subdue the flesh, terrified of thunder and lightning as the author of the *Noli Pater* evidently was, is not the

author of these "nature poems".'[18] They also ironically point to
poems evoking the delights of nature written by St Augustine of
Hippo, supposed exponent of sin-centred and fall-dominated
Roman theology in contrast to creation-centred Celtic Christianity.
'The sheer delight in nature, and the way in which such delight
elicits praise of God,' they conclude, 'is no more Celtic than
Hebrew or Roman-African.'[19]

There is one striking aspect of the outlook of the Columban
church which does seem to point to an underlying sense of the
goodness of the natural world and the created order as well as to
the importance of sign and symbol. Particular value seems to have
been attached to blessings and benedictions. Adomnán's *Life of
Columba* is full of references to monks and pilgrims coming to the
saint for a blessing. As Donald Allchin pointed out in considering
the similar prominence given to this activity in many early Welsh
Christian poems, 'to bless (*benedicere*) in its original meaning is
to speak good things, to declare the goodness which is latent in
the world around us, when that world is seen and known as the
world of God'.[20]

The emphasis of the Columban church on benediction was
part of a much wider appreciation in Celtic society of the power
of the spoken word. Both blessing and cursing were regarded
almost as physical actions which had the effect of transmitting
good or evil. In Book 2, Chapter 16 of his *Life*, Adomnán tells of
how Columba drove out a devil hiding in a milk pail by making
the saving sign of the cross over it and upbraided the young man
carrying the pail for not himself having made the sign of the cross
before he poured the milk in. We seem here to be in the realm of
superstition, pagan charms and incantations to ward off the evil
one. Or are we rather in the more mysterious realm of sacramental
theology where language and symbol are seen as having a trans-
formative power to realise the presence of Christ and turn evil

into good? Again and again Columba is portrayed by his early biographers as averting evil, whether in the form of the Loch Ness monster, a wild boar, an outbreak of plague, or a storm at sea, by making the sign of the cross, raising his hands in blessing and evoking the presence of God.

The theme of deliverance from danger looms large in many of the miracle stories associated with Columba. It is a dominant theme in two of the poems written on Iona which may well have come from his pen, *Noli Pater* with its heartfelt prayer to God to avert fire, thunder, and lightning, and *Adiutor laborantium* with its portrayal of the author as 'a little man trembling and most wretched, rowing through the infinite storm of this age'. We are reminded here of just how nasty, brutish and short life could be in the British Isles in the sixth and seventh centuries. In this context, it was not surprising that God's protective powers should be especially emphasised. God was seen in an almost literal sense as the shield and defender of those who called out in faith. St Paul's famous list in Ephesians 6.14-16 of the protective armour available to Christians – the breastplate of righteousness, the shield of faith, the helmet of salvation and the sword of the Spirit – inspired a whole genre of Irish prayers and poems, the most famous of which is that known as 'St Patrick's Breastplate' ('I bind unto myself today the strong name of the Trinity'). Alongside this *lorica* tradition (so called from the Latin word for breastplate) there developed another of encircling prayers, which possibly grew out of the old pre-Christian *caim*, and involved a circle being described around the person, family, community or place which was being entrusted to God's enfolding love. There was a strong physicality about both these styles of prayer, just as there was in Columba's action in blessing the milk churn.

This emphasis on the protective power of God, and so by analogy on the protective efficacy of prayer and of the saints, was part and parcel of a world view which saw evil manifesting itself in definite physical form. Once again, the influence of St Paul, with his evocation of 'principalities and powers ... and the spiritual hosts of wickedness in the heavenly places' (Ephesians 6.12) is very evident. This is graphically brought home in the story in Adomnán's *Life* in which Columba, praying alone on a wild part of Iona, saw 'a very black host of demons fighting against him with iron darts' and preparing to attack the monastery 'but he, single-handed, against innumerable foes of such a nature, fought with the utmost bravery, having received the armour of the apostle Paul'. The battle continued all day until 'the angels of God came to his aid' and helped drive the devils off the island. They were only banished as far as Tiree, however, where they attacked the monks of Mag Luinge with a deadly plague, the effects of which were mitigated by prayer and fasting.[21]

This dramatic account of a cosmic battle between devils and angels in which Columba took part and which resulted in such physical effects as plague takes us to the third theme which I have highlighted alongside praise and protection as characterising the theological outlook of the Columban church – that of presence. We are back once again to the New Testament world of angels and devils so vividly described by Paul and the author of Revelation. We are also not far from the world of pre-Christian Celtic mythology which was full of supernatural happenings and other worldly apparitions. If we are to believe his early biographers, Columba himself was particularly aware of supernatural presences. Adomnán noted 'how great were the bright visits of the angels made to him'.[22] As we have already noted, those around him regularly saw the saint himself surrounded by hovering angels or a halo of bright light. Alongside these visions, the members of the Columban *familia* had a highly developed sense of the close presence of the heavenly host. For them the notion of the communion of saints was no empty phrase but a vital doctrine which expressed the nearness of those who had departed from this world and passed to the next. God's protective care encompassed the dead as well as the living and his presence could be felt throughout heaven and earth, as well as across that blurred and narrow line that divided them.

There was another dimension to this theme of presence in the Columban church. It developed what I think might best be described (though not by Columba and his followers who very sensibly eschewed such jargon) as an ecclesiology of presence. Indeed, I suspect that presence might be a better word than mission to encapsulate the heart of Columba's understanding of the role and purpose of the church. We have already seen that he may not have seen himself primarily as a missionary and that the sources are conflicting as to how often and how far he went out from Iona to preach and evangelise. Much of his time seems rather to have been spent on the island guiding the monks and receiving, blessing and counselling visitors. This emphasis on pastoral care seems to have characterised the Columban church as a whole. It practised a ministry of presence, witnessing to the Lord not just by rushing around proselytising and preaching but simply by being there, available when it was needed. A major element of this ministry was the hospitality offered on Iona, symbolised by the washing of visitors' feet by the monks. It also involved a good deal of listening and a good deal of quiet and patient healing of broken souls. The Iona community offered pastoral care not just to the many visitors who came to the island from far afield but also to the local population. This seems to have been a general characteristic of Irish monasteries. Even someone as sceptical about the concept of Celtic Christianity as Wendy Davies concedes that the pastoral outreach to the local community in terms of baptism, burial and spiritual counselling was almost certainly stronger in the Christian communities of Ireland, Scotland and Wales than in Continental monasteries. Indeed, she is even prepared to accept that this may count as a distinct characteristic of Celtic Christianity as a whole.[23]

This pastoral ministry of presence was closely bound up with the central role accorded to penitence in the Columban church. Many of those who found their way to Iona were misfits and outcasts, consumed with feelings of guilt, remorse and low self-esteem. Often they had committed serious crimes for which they could not forgive themselves. On the island they experienced the healing power of the *medicamenta penitentiae* (the medicine of penance), a combination of penitential discipline and spiritual counselling. We are not talking here about an almost mechanical device of confession and absolution such as the sacrament of penance became in the later medieval church. Rather, Columba and his contemporaries had a deep understanding of the human predicament of alienation, self-doubt and separation from God and from other people. They responded with a programme of healing which tackled the whole person, body, mind and soul, and which was predicated on the need for repeated forgiveness and assurance of acceptance by God.

Penitential discipline was far from being soft. The *Irish Penitentials*, which form the largest single category of document to have come down to us from the so-called 'golden age' of Celtic Christianity, are full of severe punishments for what often seem to our eyes trivial lapses and faults and enjoin a constant state of watchfulness and rigorous self-control. They belong, of course, to a monastic context and it should not be forgotten that they apply first and foremost to those who have taken vows and are living voluntarily under a strict rule. The principle of penitence spread out beyond the monastic *vallum*, however. Much of the work of Columba and his fellow monks on Iona seems to have involved handing out *medicamenta penitentiae* to lay visitors who came in desperate search of healing and wholeness. It could be harsh. An Irishman called Lugaid who had slept with his own mother was told that he must spend twelve years among the British, 'repenting with tears of remorse', and never return to his native land. Other penitents were regularly banished to Tiree for seven years to live as anchorites, a term which interestingly comes from a Coptic word meaning displaced persons who have lost their place in society.

Tough though it undoubtedly was, the strong penitential discipline administered by the Columban church also had great healing power. Hugh Connolly, author of a book on the *Irish Penitentials*, describes them as 'handbooks for confessors or physicians of souls who used them in order to steer the faithful away from behaviour which was spiritually harmful, to heal them from the effects of sin, to instruct them in the virtues which were to be sought after and to indicate a means by which this virtuous state might be achieved'.[24] Sensitive pastors that they were, Columba and his contemporaries combined prescription, instruction, advice and empathy in seeking to cure sick souls. Crucial to their approach was the role of the *anamchara*, or soul friend, who combined the functions of cellmate, spiritual counsellor, father confessor and buddy. Disappointingly, Columba's various biographers give virtually no indication of the saint's dealings with his own *anamchara* although they tell us enough to make it clear that he had one and that he himself acted in that capacity for others. The rule associated with his name also alludes to the practice when it enjoins monks to perform their vigils 'from eve to eve under the direction of another person'. There is no doubt that the system of soul friends operated within the monastic community on Iona. We can be less sure how far it extended to the local community and to visitors.

Penitence was also about the propagation of justice and the

righting of wrongs. The regime prescribed for penitents was not just designed to address their guilt but also to help their victims and provide reparations for injuries suffered. Here we get a glimpse of Columba as judge, administrator and upholder of law and order as well as priest and pastor. We are, indeed, reminded of his wider political interests and his strong commitment to the rule of law and the replacement of feuding chieftains and warlords by more settled and peaceful systems of authority. Under both its founder and his successors, Iona played a key role in supporting and legitimising the rule of just and fair monarchs and in promoting the institution of kingship. It was very much a community in touch with secular society and not just a secluded sacred ghetto keeping its distance from the nasty world of politics. At the same time it was also very much a provisional community, avoiding both the triumphalism and the institutional paralysis that comes with building up rigid permanent structures. The ministry of presence that to some extent defined the ethos of the Columban church did not make it a static body. Rather it was a church that was constantly on the move, physically as well as spiritually. Monks on Iona did not take a vow of stability as their counterparts in Benedictine houses did. Many seem to have served as itinerant clergy going round the country equipped with the basic tools of their trade – Gospel book, psalter, prayer book, hand bell and portable altar.

Provisionality was very much the hallmark of Columban ecclesiology. There were no stone buildings on Iona, nor indeed in the Irish and British monasteries as a whole. Ninian's decision to build a stone church at *Candida Casa* at Whithorn was exceptional, as Bede noted in his history. Like most of their contemporaries, Columba and his monks were content to worship God in a simple wooden church, a wattle and daub hut or in the open air at the foot of a cross. There was no sense of building a monument that would last for centuries as the Romans had done and the Normans were later to do. In this provisionality we perhaps find another distinguishing characteristic of Celtic Christianity as a whole, identified by Ian Finlay in his life of Columba: 'A Roman saw every achievement in terms of a stone monument, whereas a Celt barely understood the idea of a monument at all ... The Roman bent nature to his purposes, the Celt adapted himself to nature.'[25] We are brought back to the theme of pilgrimage which we have already encountered in looking at the reasons for Columba's journey to Iona in 563. The Columban church was a pilgrim church, a community and movement as much as an institution or establishment. It sat lightly to the world, behaving as one who had no abiding city here.

Several different elements went into the motif of pilgrimage that perhaps provides the best key for unlocking the distinctive ethos and character of the Columban church. There was the influence of the desert fathers with their austere and ascetic disciplines as they sought to distance themselves from worldly comforts and distractions and find God in the wilderness. There was the sense of life as a journey, of the need constantly to be prepared to discard unwanted and outdated baggage and to change, progressing through harms and dangers. There was the emphasis on white martyrdom and witnessing to Christ through a life of exile and self-abandonment. There was, too, the strong feeling of community, solidarity and companionship in suffering so that, in Hugh Connolly's words, 'the emphasis is placed not so much on the saving judgement or salutary medicine but on the fraternal witness and compassion of the *anamchara*'.[26] There is much here that pre-echoes modern theology in its concern with patripassianism, God's sharing in the suffering of the world, and its insistence that it is only the wounded healer who can bring real wholeness to the broken. Columba and his contemporaries never

felt that their spiritual journeys had ended in this world, nor that
they had reached their destinations. They felt themselves and the
church which they built up, but did not idolise, to be provisional,
imperfect, ever travelling on to new ways of expressing and understanding the Gospel and new glimpses of God's glory. This sense
is beautifully encapsulated in an old Irish poem attributed to Columba but almost certainly from a later hand which weaves
together the themes of pilgrimage, presence and protection:

> *The path I walk, Christ walks it.*
> *May the land in which I am be without sorrow.*
> *May the Trinity protect me wherever I stay,*
> *Father, Son and Holy Spirit.*
> *Bright angels walk with me – dear presence – in every dealing.*
> *In every dealing I pray them*
> *that no one's poison may reach me.*
> *The ninefold people of heaven of holy cloud,*
> *the tenth force of the stout earth.*
> *Favourable company, they come with me,*
> *so that the Lord may not be angry with me.*
> *May I arrive at every place, may I return home;*
> *may the way in which I spend be a way without loss.*
> *May every path before me be smooth,*
> *man, woman and child welcome me.*
> *A truly good journey!*
> *Well does the fair Lord show us a course, a path.*[27]

Notes

1   George Campbell, 8th Duke of Argyll, *Iona*, p.41
2   Donald Meek, review of *IONA: The Earliest Poetry of a Celtic Monastery* in *New Blackfriars*, no. 76 (1995), pp.467-68
3   Wendy Davies, 'The Myth of the Celtic church' in Nancy Edwards and Alan Lane (eds), *The Early Church in Wales and the West* (Oxbow Books, Oxford, 1992), p.11
4   Jocelyn Toynbee, 'Christianity in Roman Britain', *Journal of the British Archaeological Association*, no.16 (1953), p.24
5   Thomas Owen Clancy and Gilbert Márkus, *IONA*, p.8
6   Sally Foster, *Picts, Gaels and Scots* (Historic Scotland & B.T.Batsford, London, 1996), p.83
7   Archie Duncan, *Scotland: The Making of the Kingdom* (Oliver and Boyd, Edinburgh, 1975), p.66
8   Clancy and Márkus, *IONA*, p.222
9   John Ryan, *Irish Monasticism* (Four Courts Press, Dublin, 1992), pp.410-11
10 Ryan, *Irish Monasticism*, p.409
11 The *Rule of Columcille* as printed in the appendix of Samuel Stone, *Lays of Iona and Other Poems* (Longmans, Green & Co., London, 1897), pp.112
12 *Ibid.*, p.110
13 *Ibid.*, p.112
14 Ryan, *Irish Monasticism*, p.307
15 Clancy and Márkus, *IONA*, p.80
16 On the Welsh tradition of praise poetry see Donald Allchin, *Praise Above All: Discovering the Welsh Tradition* (University of Wales Press, Cardiff, 1991) and Oliver Davies, *Celtic Christianity in Early Medieval Wales* (University of Wales Press, Cardiff, 1995)
17 Alexander Carmichael, *Carmina Gadelica* (Floris Books, Edinburgh, 1992), p.30
18 Clancy and Márkus, *IONA*, p.90
19 *Ibid.*, pp.92-93

20   Allchin, *Praise Above All*, p.6
21   *Life of Columba*, p.83-4
22   *Life of Columba*, p.101
23   Davies, 'The Myth of the Celtic church', p.15
24   Hugh Connolly, *The Irish Penitentials* (Four Courts Press, Dublin, 1995), p.21
25   Ian Finlay, *Columba*, p.167
26   Connolly, *The Irish Penitentials*, p.178
27   James Carney, 'Three Old Irish Poems' in *Ériu* (Dublin: Royal Irish Academy, 1971) pp.27-8

Four

The legacy of Columba

Columba's influence did not come to an end with his death in 597. Indeed, he became an even more important figure in death than he had been in life. Thanks to the expansion of the monastic *familia* centred on Iona into eastern and southern Scotland and northern England, and the steady growth of the political power of the kingdom of Dál Riata, the cult of Columba flourished during the seventh and eighth centuries. Armies carried his relics into battle as talismans to secure victory while the invocation of his name or prayer through him was said to avert danger. Miracle stories testified to his posthumous powers of protection.

Unlike other Celtic saints who often had to wait several hundred years before their lives were written up and celebrated, Columba was eulogised almost immediately after his death. The *Amra Choluimb Chille*, written around 600 and attributed to Dallán Forgaill, an Irish poet who clearly had access to material from Iona, emphasised his asceticism and celebrated the life of a scholar whose interests stretched well beyond biblical exegesis and theology into the realms of mathematics and astronomy. The conscious development of a Columba cult on Iona seems to have begun with a systematic trawl to collect hagiographical material by Ségéne, the fifth abbot of Iona (623-52). Among its results was the production by his nephew, Cumméne, of a *Book of the Miracles of Columba*. Although only a tiny fragment survives, it shows a shift in focus from Columba's actual life and achievements towards his supernatural encounters and posthumous miracles. The two poems written around 650 by Beccán mac Luigdech, a hermit associated with the Iona family of monasteries, make much of the saint's posthumous power, deriving from his position in the hierarchy of heaven, to protect those who call on him in trouble or danger.

The classic *Vita* written by Adomnán, abbot of Iona from 679 to 704, marked a decisive final stage in Columba's unofficial 'canonisation'. As we have seen, its emphasis was on the saint's

supernatural and miraculous powers. Adomnán included posthumous miracles, including some which he had witnessed himself
and suggested that actual physical contact with Columba's relics
was not necessary in order to harness his protective powers – it
was enough to mention his name in the context of prayer or
praise. He recounted how a group of 'wicked men of lewd conver-
sation and men of blood' were saved from the hands of their
enemies by singing hymns in praise of Columba. 'They safely
escaped through through the flames, the swords and the spears;
and, strange to tell, a few of those only who despised these commemorations of the holy man, and refused to join in the hymns
perished in the assault of the enemy.'[1] Many of the miracles
described by Adomnán were set in Pictland and point to the
superiority of the Gaelic-speaking Scots over the Picts as well as
of Christianity over paganism. By his time Gaelic-speaking monks
from Iona were penetrating the Pictish strongholds of northern
and eastern Scotland. Columba was adopted as the patron of this
movement of Gaelic colonisation and taken up by the rulers of
Dál Riata as they extended their influence northwards and eastwards across the Scottish mainland.

It is significant that the cult of Columba was developed and
encouraged primarily by his successors on Iona. The monastery
which he had founded there remained the hub of the extensive
and growing Columban *paruchia* in Ireland and Scotland during
the two centuries following his death. Columba's successors as
abbots of Iona, the great majority of whom were members of his
own family, maintained the high and exacting standards that he
had set. Writing in the 730s, Bede noted that they were 'renowned
for their continence, their love of God, and observance of monastic rules. It is true they employed doubtful cycles in fixing the
time of the great festival, as having none to bring them the synodal
decrees for the observance of Easter, by reason of their being so

far away from the rest of the world; but they earnestly practised such works of piety and chastity as they could learn from the Prophets, the Gospels and the Apostolic writings.'[2] Members of the community that Columba had founded on Iona played a key part in the evangelisation of northern and eastern Scotland along with other British and Irish missionary monks like Ternan and Maelrubha. By Adomnán's time there were churches in Aberdeenshire and Angus associated with the Columban *familia*. Bede is clear that Iona ruled the Pictish monasteries and a modern historian of early Scotland, Alfred Smyth, is equally certain that Columba's foundation provided the parent culture for Pictish Christianity and that 'Iona acted as the great disseminator of ideas and motifs throughout Pictland'.[3] Royal patronage almost certainly greatly helped this process. There is evidence that by the late seventh century the kings of Dál Riata had extended their rule eastwards from modern Argyllshire to take in areas of central Scotland previously under Pictish control.

It was also royal patronage that directly effected the most important extension of the Iona *familia* and brought the cult of Columba into England. Indeed, Columba's own kingmaking activities may well have laid the foundations for the mission to Northumbria which was to provide northern England with its own set of Celtic saints. It is certainly striking that, in the words of Ian Muirhead, 'Iona's most successful enterprise came, not through self-initiated mission but through a royal invitation'.[4] The story began with the escape to Iona of the young Anglian prince Oswald in 617 when his father was ousted from the Northumbrian throne. During his sojourn on the island, which seems to have lasted for seventeen years, he received not just sanctuary but also instruction in the Christian faith and he was baptised there. In 634 Oswald succeeded in wresting back the Northumbrian throne after fighting a battle against the Welsh king Cadwollan who had seized it the previous year. According to Adomnán, during the night before the battle Oswald had a vision of Columba who promised him his protection and prophesied that Cadwollan and his forces would be routed. Duly victorious, one of Oswald's first actions on becoming king of Northumbria was to ask Ségéne, the abbot of Iona, to send him a missionary bishop to establish a church in his extensive kingdom which stretched from the banks of the Forth to Yorkshire. The choice fell on Aidan, who founded his first monastery on the island of Lindisfarne, strategically situated near the royal stronghold of Bamburgh but also remote enough to be a place of prayer and retreat.

Under the ultimate authority of Iona and very much part of the Columban *paruchia*, Lindisfarne became the base for the evangelisation of Northumbria and also much of eastern and central England. It spawned a large number of daughter houses including those at Whitby, Coldingham, Lastingham and Melrose. Bede noted that, in the wake of Aidan, many monks from Scots Dál Riata came 'into Britain and to those English kingdoms over which Oswald reigned, preaching the word of faith with great devotion'.[5] They included the first two bishops of Mercia, Diuma and Cellach. Aidan also trained native Northumbrians for work among the Angles, among them two brothers still remembered in English church dedications – Chad who established his base at Lichfield, and Cedd who worked among the east Saxons and set up monasteries at Tilbury and Bradwell-on-Sea. Perhaps the best known of the products of this branch of the Columban monastic empire was St Cuthbert whose career, in the words of Alfred Smyth, 'represented a happy marriage between older Celtic and newer forms of Anglo-Saxon Christianity in northern Bernicia'.[6] Born in the Borders, he entered the monastery at Melrose in 651 and moved to Lindisfarne as prior in 664, spending the last thirty-three years of his life combining the running of a busy and complex island monastery with periods of solitary retreat and prayer, just as Columba had done a century earlier.

The extension of the Columban church into Northumbria seems to have coincided with a low point in the fortunes of the kingdom of Dál Riata. Indeed, the two events may be connected. The rulers of Dál Riata faced an increasingly hostile challenge from their southern neighbours, the Strathclyde Britons, and accepted Northumbrian protection and overlordship from around 637. It seems quite likely that the arrival of monks from Iona in Lothian and Northumbria was connected with this new political arrangement. Expansion into the lands of the Angles was to bring its own problems for the Columban church in the form of tension with the more Romanised church which had developed in the south of England in the aftermath of St Augustine's mission to Canterbury in 597. This was the background to the Synod of Whitby, at which representatives of each church met to debate their differences. Oswald's brother Oswy, who had succeeded him on the Northumbrian throne in 642, had married a Kentish princess, Eanfled, who had been brought up in Roman ways. Specifically, she was accustomed to celebrating Easter according to a relatively new calendar which had been adopted in Rome in place of the old one which was still in use on Iona and in many parts of northern Ireland. This had unfortunate consequences at court. In the words of Bede, 'it sometimes happened in those times that Easter was twice celebrated in one year; and that when the king, having ended his fast, was keeping Easter, the queen and her followers were still fasting, and celebrating Palm Sunday'.[7] Wishing to end this anomaly and secure a single agreed method for calculating Easter which would pertain throughout his kingdom, Oswy called a synod at Whitby in 664. The main protagonists were Colman, abbot and bishop of Lindisfarne on the Columban side, and, on the Roman side, Wilfrid, abbot of Ripon who had trained at Lindisfarne but had subsequently visited Rome and converted to its practices.

The debate at Whitby was recorded in detail by Bede. Much of the argument hinged around the authority of Columba and showed the extent to which his example was still being appealed to more than 150 years after his death. Wilfrid began his case by maintaining that the new way of calculating Easter was accepted by the church not just in Rome but in Africa, Asia, Egypt, Greece and everywhere else except among the *Scoti* 'and their accomplices in obstinacy, I mean the Picts and the Britons, who in these, the two remotest islands of the Ocean, foolishly attempt to oppose all the rest of the world'. Colman retorted that it was inconceivable that 'our most reverend Father Columba and his successors, men beloved by God, who kept Easter after the same manner, judged or acted contrary to the Divine writings when there were many among them, whose sanctity was attested by heavenly signs and miracles which they wrought; whom I, for my part, doubt not to be saints, and whose life, customs, and discipline I never cease to follow'. Wilfrid responded by patronisingly describing Columba and his followers as misguided and ignorant men 'who loved God with rude simplicity but pious intent', and then produced the trump card always used to support the Roman church's claim to supremacy: 'Even if that Columba of yours (and, I may say, ours also, if he was Christ's servant) was a holy man and powerful in miracles, yet could he be preferred before the most blessed chief of the Apostles, to whom our Lord said, "Thou art Peter, and upon this rock I will build my church, and the gates of hell shall not prevail against it, and I will give unto thee the keys of the kingdom of Heaven?"'[8]

This appeal to Petrine authority seems to have won the day. Oswy ruled in favour of the Roman method of calculating Easter and also declared his desire that the Northumbrian church should follow Rome in other matters of ecclesiastical order and usage which differed from Irish practice, the most noticeable of which was the way in which monks cut their hair. Colman resigned his abbacy and see and returned to his native Ireland with a number of the monks from Lindisfarne. The Easter controversy dragged on for several more decades. Adomnán was converted to the Roman system of dating Easter in 688 but could not persuade the monks on Iona to join him. Some historians have suggested that he wrote his *Life of Columba* to prove his Columban credentials and his attachment to the founder in the hope that this might persuade the Iona community that it was not a matter of disloyalty to abandon his way of doing things in this particular instance. The extent to which Iona's stubborn refusal to break with tradition led to increasing isolation was highlighted around 717 when the Pictish king Nechthan expelled members of the Columban *familia* from his territories and announced that from henceforth the church in Pictland would follow Roman practices. He was probably motivated partly by his desire to keep in with Northumbria but also by the influence of an English monk, Egbert. Shortly afterwards, and possibly as a response to Nechthan's ban, the *paruchia Columbae*, together with most other monasteries in northern Ireland, finally gave up their long-cherished traditions and adopted the Roman method of calculating Easter and the Roman style of tonsure.

The Synod of Whitby has often been seen as marking a turning point in the history of Christianity in the British Isles. It is very tempting to interpret it as signalling the crushing of the gentle, anarchic spirit of Celtic Christianity by the authoritarian bureaucracy of the Roman Church, and the way Bede writes it up rather encourages this temptation. In her book *The Celtic Alternative*, Shirley Toulson argued that 664 was a more important date in British history than 1066.[9] In reality, the significance of the Synod itself was limited although it is certainly true that it symbolised the way things were going for some of the distinctive features of the Columban church. Perhaps the key question which divided proponents of Irish and Roman church organisation was whether Britain should have a federation of monastic *paruchiae* or a diocesan system run by bishops. This was not on the agenda at Whitby and does not seem to have been discussed at the Synod. Here, however, as over the dating of Easter and the favoured hairstyle for monks, the writing was on the wall for the Columban way of doing things and for a church which looked increasingly provincial and conservative in its ethos. In the opinion of the distinguished historian Ian Cowan, the church in Scotland was 'consistently moving onwards towards a diocesan system from the eighth century onwards'.[10]

Back on Iona, sometime between 730 and 753 Columba's original simple underground grave was opened and his remains reinterred, together with his sacred bell, books, staff and tunic, in an elaborate elevated casket shrine on the site of the later chapel which can still be seen today to the left of the great west door of Iona Abbey. The pretext for this re-enshrinement may have been the takeover of Dál Riata by the Picts under King Oengus. It was almost certainly also inspired by the broader cult of the saints which swept over Christian Europe in this period, producing a heightened sense of their miraculous powers and the continued corporeal presence exerted through their relics, and greatly stimulating pilgrimage to their shrines.

The enshrinement of Columba's relics seems to have been accompanied by the development of a processional route designed to lead pilgrims from their landing place near the present ferry terminal on Iona up to Columba's shrine through a ritual landscape and along a street of the dead modelled perhaps on the route to the Church of the Holy Sepulchre in Jerusalem known as the

Via Dolorosa. Reinforcing the sense of a deliberately planned landscape of death, this route also became the way in which the coffins of those who were buried on Iona were brought to the graveyard at the *Reilig Odhrain* which had been established outside the monastic precincts in the previous century.

The creation of this processional way reflected a renewed interest in dramatising and revivifying the faith by encouraging people to walk symbolically in the footsteps of Christ on the way to his crucifixion at Calvary, also shown by the development of the practice of establishing Stations of the Cross in churches. This new emphasis on walking as well as talking the faith also chimed in with the interest in sacred space and holy places aroused by works such as Adomnán's *De Locis Sanctis*, written on Iona at the end of the seventh century. The cult of the saints stimulated the Christian faithful to make pilgrimages to saints' shrines in a quest to connect with their power through touching their relics. It also inspired a more radical desire to die and to be buried near saints. This became particularly important with respect to Columba and Iona, reinforcing the already strong belief that one should go west to die. Many would have echoed the sentiments of a statement attributed to Adomnán and now stencilled on the wall in the entrance to the cloisters of Iona Abbey: 'If I be destined to die in Iona, it were a merciful leave taking. I know not under the blue sky a better spot for death.' Even if you did not manage to die there, you could be buried there, especially if you were rich. Being laid to rest near Columba meant that you were already close to God and it supposedly made the journey to heaven shorter. In that way, Iona became important and attractive as a gateway to the afterlife. Several Irish kings and princes were recorded as journeying 'in pilgrimage and penance' to spend their last years there in the late eighth century.

This was the context for the laying out of several of the features that can still very clearly be seen by visitors to Iona today – notably the cemetery at the Reilig Odhráin and the Street of the Dead which runs to and through it and on to the site of Columba's shrine. It made Iona in a very conscious way a landscape of the dead, both in terms of the continuing corporeal and spiritual presence of Columba and other holy figures buried there and also in its popularity as a final resting place for many influential and wealthy figures. There is now considerable doubt as to whether Iona deserves its accolade as the burial place of Scotland's early kings but it did undoubtedly become a favourite location for the great and the good to have their final resting place, as the many coffin roads to its shores testify.

The most visible and enduring legacy of Iona's makeover as a ritual landscape were the four high standing crosses erected between the mid-eighth and early ninth centuries along the processional pilgrim way to Columba's shrine and possibly intended as prayer stations and symbols of protection and presence delineating sacred space. It is perhaps no coincidence that they were erected during the period when the Christian Gaels of Argyll were being attacked by the pagan Vikings. The first Viking attack on Iona was in 795 and there were increasingly ferocious raids thereafter, with 68 members of the monastic community being killed in 806, and a monk named Blathmac being put to death in 825 for refusing to divulge the whereabouts of the precious casket containing Columba's relics which he had hidden under a mound. It is possible that one of these massacres is commemorated in the Gaelic name for the bay to the south of Iona's main pier, Port nam Mairtear. It could suggest martyrdom, as its English translation, Martyrs Bay, suggests, but it could also simply mean 'Bay of the Dead' and indicate that this was where coffins were landed for burial on the island.

Iona was now too vulnerable to remain as the centre of the

Columban *familia* and most of the monks moved to a new monastery which had been built at Kells in County Meath in the centre of Ireland well away from any danger of attack. A few monks remained to brave the Viking raids on Iona but Kells, to which treasures, including Columba's reliquary, illuminated manuscripts and metalwork, were removed, achieved primacy within the Columban *paruchia*. Significantly, its abbots continued to style themselves abbots of Iona. With the sea no longer a safe highway but rather a dangerous barrier to communication, Iona became increasingly cut off from other Columban foundations and the centre of gravity within the *familia* shifted to Ireland.

Meanwhile, on the Scottish mainland the warring Picts and Scots gradually developed a closer relationship during the ninth century. This may partly have been brought about as a response to the common danger of Viking invasion but it may also have been the result of successful military operations by the Scottish Gaels effectively subduing the Picts. The figure generally credited with bringing them together and with being the first ruler of a joint Scottish-Pictish kingdom, Kenneth Mac Ailpín, was of mixed descent, his father coming from the ruling family of Dál Riata, the mac Gabráins, and his mother being a Pictish princess. King of Dál Riata from 840 and of the Picts from 843, he went on to achieve ascendancy over the lands around the Tweed which had formerly been part of the Anglian kingdom of Bernicia. By marrying his daughter to the king of Strathclyde he also came to exercise considerable influence over Scotland's fourth major ethnic and tribal grouping. Thanks to his own Dál Riatan background, Kenneth Mac Ailpín was a fervent devotee of Columba and as the first ruler of what was to become the united kingdom of Alba, the precursor of modern Scotland, he gave a considerable boost both to the saint's cult and to his church. Around 849 he moved those of Columba's relics which had not already gone to

Kells to Dunkeld in Perthshire which he established as the ecclesiastical capital of his new kingdom.

In death, as in life, Columba was enlisted in the cause of dynastic rivalries and political battles. Rivalry between Picts and Scots was not ended with the rule of Kenneth Mac Ailpín. His successors as kings of Alba gradually extended their control over the more northerly Pictish territories, helped, in the words of Sally Foster, by 'the aggression of a revitalised Gaelic Church, promoting the language of St Columba'.[11] A carved stone near Forres dating from the late ninth or early tenth century, which seems to commemorate a significant victory of the Scots over the men of Moray, perhaps one of the last outposts of Pictland, has a scene showing a Mac Ailpín king being crowned apparently in the presence of St Columba and St Andrew. Columba's crozier, or staff, was carried as a protective device by Scottish armies facing the invading Viking armies in the tenth century. In a similar way his psalter, which had been taken to Ireland along with other relics, was encased in a silver casket and paraded by the Uí Néills in all their military adventures. The O'Donnells, successors to the Uí Néills, became hereditary keepers of the *Cathach*, which was believed to secure victory in battle, and they continued parading it until the sixteenth century.

Not all the Vikings and their Norse descendants were hostile to Columba. An increasing number converted to Christianity and settled in the Hebridean islands through the tenth and eleventh centuries. In 980 Olaf Sihtricsson, who had been Norse king of Northumbria and Dublin, retired to Iona in 'penitence and pilgrimage'. When Magnus Barelegs, King of Norway, raided both the Outer and Inner Hebrides in 1098, he spared Iona, halting on the threshold of the chapel containing Columba's shrine and ordering his men not to enter or deface it. For the pagan Norse, Columba had some of the qualities of the Viking god Odin. Several of those who became Christian built churches dedicated to him as far afield as Iceland.

The small monastic community still resident on Iona received a boost from Queen Margaret of Scotland who was possibly responsible for ordering the construction around 1080 of the first permanent stone place of worship, and the earliest surviving ecclesiastical building on the island, St Oran's Chapel. Herself deeply pious and an admirer of the eremitical and austere tradition of Columba and his fellow Irish monks, Queen Margaret and her husband, Malcolm Canmore, who ruled from 1058 to 1093, are generally credited with the anglicising and Romanising of the Scottish church. Unable to speak Gaelic, she introduced many English customs and practices to the Scottish court and relied heavily for ecclesiastical advice on her chaplain, Turgot, who had been sent to Scotland by Lanfranc, Archbishop of Canterbury. Possibly under his influence, the Norman system of territorial diocesan organisation already in place in England was introduced north of the border. Scottish monasteries, including those set up by the reforming Culdee movement from Ireland, were reorganised along Continental lines. Margaret was behind the foundation of the first Benedictine monastery in Scotland which was established at Dunfermline Abbey in 1072. Benedictine monks came to Iona in 1203, effectively ending more than 600 years of a distinctive Columban church presence there. Their abbey, which continued to call itself Columba's monastery, flourished for the next three and a half centuries until the Reformation, with a steady stream of pilgrims coming to venerate Columba's shrine.

In Ireland, as in Scotland, the Columban church largely disappeared as a distinct entity during the twelfth century. Following the Norman invasion of Ireland in 1169, the monasteries throughout the country were brought under episcopal control and, like other similar federations which crossed diocesan boundaries and owed allegiance to an abbot rather than a bishop, the Columban *paruchia* disintegrated. The territorially organised diocesan system which St Patrick had first tried to introduce seven centuries earlier had at last prevailed. Patrick's own star was also in the ascendant as the see which he had established at Armagh was recognised as having primacy in the Irish church as a whole and his position secured as the nation's patron saint. Attempts to promote Columba's candidacy in his native land came to naught, not least because the power of his main supporters, the northern Uí Néills, was in decline.

The new nation of Scotland might well have been expected to adopt Columba as its patron saint. Certainly his stock remained high long after the particular style and structure of church with which his name had been associated had disappeared. His crozier, which was kept at Dunkeld, was carried as a protective device by Scottish armies facing the invading Viking armies at Corbridge in 918 and became known as the *Cathbhuaidh*, or battle talisman. In 1123 a monastery dedicated to him was founded on the island of Inchcolm in the Firth of Forth. From it comes the *Inchcolm Antiphoner*, one of the most important manuscripts in the history of plainchant which contains a remarkably beautiful service of commemoration for St Columba who is described and invoked as '*Spes Scotorum*' (the Hope of the Scots). It includes some antiphons, with an altogether freer and more ethereal sound than that of Gregorian chant, which musicologists feel may belong to the seventh or eighth century and take us back to the sound of Christian worship around Columba's own time. Much of the music in the *Antiphoner* is almost certainly of later provenance: the manuscript in which it is found dates from the fourteenth century and it includes a *Benedictus* which calls on 'Father Columba, the glory of our national tradition' to 'save this choir which is praising you from attack by the English'. We know that English pirates plundered

Inchcolm Abbey in 1336.[12]

Another fine piece of art associated with the cult of Columba is the Monymusk Reliquary, also known by its Gaelic name 'Breccbenach', a small wooden box decorated with bronze and silver plates, semi-precious stones and enamels. Apparently built to house a bone of the saint, it was entrusted to the abbot of Arbroath by King William I of Scotland so that it might be available for blessing the royal troops in battle. On the eve of the decisive battle in 1314 when Robert the Bruce confronted the English army under King Edward II of England at Bannockburn, it was paraded before the Scottish forces and fully lived up to its reputation as a bringer of victory.

Devotion to Columba throughout the Middle Ages, not least among the Lords of the Isles, led to numerous chapels, churches, wells and other natural and human-made features being dedicated to him. He was hailed as a protector by the Scots as a whole when they faced their enemies. The Norse also enlisted him in their efforts to retain their hold over the islands off Argyll. In 1249 King Alexander II of Scotland, lying off the island of Kerrera on his way to attack King Haakon's Norse fleet in the Hebrides, was told in a vision by Columba, who appeared to him as a 'frowning figure, very bald in front', to return home. He ignored the advice and was promptly stricken with a fever. Landed on Kerrera, Alexander died on the eastern shore at a place which is still called Ach-an-Righ, or the Field of the King. Norwegian sources credit the saint's posthumous intervention with preventing an attack on the Hebrides.

Despite the extent of his cult and his enlistment as protector of the Scots, Columba was not to become the new nation's patron saint. A rival cult of Andrew the apostle developed in the late eighth or ninth century among the Picts of north east Fife, having almost certainly originated in Northumbria where it had been strongly championed by Wilfrid, the chief protagonist of the pro-

Roman side at the Synod of Whitby. Andrew was championed by the Picts as a counter to the Scots' support for the Gaelic Columba and this almost certainly lay behind the emergence of the story around this time that his relics had been brought to Fife by a monk called Rule or Regulus in the fifth century. There was certainly a geographical dimension to the contest between the two saints' supporters. While Columba reigned supreme in the west of Scotland, Andrew's cult spread in the east from its original base at Kinrymont, the site of the modern city of St Andrews where first a church and then a great cathedral were built to house his supposed relics. As the centre of ecclesiastical gravity in Scotland shifted eastwards, first from Iona to Dunkeld, and then to St Andrews, so the apostle gained ground over the Irish monk. Queen Margaret of Scotland gave a boost to the cult of St Andrew by establishing a ferry crossing across the Forth for pilgrims visiting his shrine.

It took a long time before Andrew rather than Columba was universally recognised and indubitably established as Scotland's patron saint. His popularity rose slowly but steadily throughout the Middle Ages, helped by the emergence of the Archbishopric of St Andrews with undisputed jurisdiction over a single independent Scottish ecclesiastical province.[13] Andrew gained in stature through his association with the cause of Scottish independence and in the diagonal cross of the saltire he provided a peculiarly powerful visual symbol of Scottish nationhood. A seal produced by the guardians appointed to rule Scotland after King Alexander III's death in 1286 carrying the words '*Andreas dux esto Scotis compatriotis*' (Andrew, be leader of the Scots compatriots) is often taken to mark the beginning of Andrew's reign as official patron saint. Ultimately, the 'establishment' figure, backed by the ecclesiastical and civil hierarchy, won.

Yet even after Andrew's position was secure, Columba

remained an infinitely more popular figure among the Scottish people. He was seen in many country districts as the special protector of cattle and his name was linked to a plant, also known as St John's wort, which was much valued for its healing properties. During the late fifteenth century depictions of 24 of his miracles were painted on the wall behind the high altar of Dunkeld Cathedral and two statues of the saint were erected in the nave. Around 1500 priests in Dunkeld were giving local people water into which one of Columba's bones had been dipped to protect them from plague. Successful repulsions of Sassenach incursions following the invocation of his protection in prayers suggested that while no longer the nation's official patron saint, he was still second to none in his ability to protect the Scots against the English. There were at least 55 churches across Scotland dedicated to Columba by the beginning of the sixteenth century, far more than to any other Irish or British saint, or, indeed, to Andrew.

The Reformation did not diminish Columba's popularity in Scotland even if it curbed the cults associated with his relics and protective powers. Scottish Reformers enthusiastically recruited him as a Proto-Protestant in their efforts to prove that the early Celtic church had been fundamentally anti-Roman. The *History of the Kirk in Scotland*, written by David Calderwood following his return to Scotland in 1625 after a period of exile for attacking monarchical interference in the forms of worship of the Kirk, lauded Columba for his austere life and for the fact that his monks on Iona 'were far different from the monks which arose after in corrupter times'. Calderwood could not resist pointing out that Columba was 'a presbyter, not a bishop', a fact that endeared him to many Presbyterians.

It could, indeed, be argued that it is among the Protestant communities of the Highlands and Islands that the distinctive precepts of Columban Christianity have been most clearly and closely followed in later centuries. Donald Meek has characterised Highland religion as involving 'a profoundly serious approach to worship, an awareness of the centrality of Scripture, respect for preaching, the observance of the Sabbath and an overall awareness of the sovereignty of God'. He points to the central place of the Psalms in worship, respect for supernatural experience and 'a pervasive sense of another level of existence beyond the physical'. He also mentions a traditional emphasis on oral transmission of information, song and story which has produced 'a massive capacity for memorisation, harnessed skilfully by catechists and preachers', and an innate conservatism and capacity for retrospection leading to 'a natural tendency to admire the leaders, models and practices of an earlier age', especially the heroes of both the Christian and pre-Christian past.[14] All of these were strong characteristics of Columban Christianity. There is a distinct echo of Columba's mixture of deep piety, genuine humility and strong, somewhat autocratic leadership qualities in the make-up of that formidable spiritual élite known as 'The Men' who wielded such influence in Highland and Island Presbyterianism during the eighteenth and nineteenth centuries. Like the saint of Iona, they combined a sensitive awareness of the supernatural, a deep prayerfulness and a strong personal charisma with a powerful regulatory role in the local community, directing the overall religious, moral and social tone of their localities. Some were said, like Columba, to possess gifts of prophecy.[15]

The legacy of Columban Christianity is particularly clear in the rich and distinctive body of Gaelic religious verse produced in the Highlands in the eighteenth and nineteenth centuries. The *Dain Spioradail* (spiritual songs) and *Laoidhean Spioradail* (spiritual hymns) written by Dugald Buchanan of Perthshire, Peter Grant of Strathspey, John MacDonald of Ferintosh and other evangelical Presbyterians and Baptists exhibit several of the characteristics that we have already noted in the verses of Columba and his successors on Iona. There is a similar emphasis on the sovereignty and majesty of God, displayed through his works in creation and illustrated through the vivid physical imagery of the Psalms, on the importance of neighbourliness and community, on God's protective powers and the utter dependence of humanity on Him, and on the theme of spiritual pilgrimage.

These evangelical Highland poets shared the conviction so strongly held in the Columban church that faith should be sung as well as spoken, expressed in poetry rather than prose and communicated through symbol, image and metaphor as much as through concept, reason and argument. Their work also involved a similar intermingling of the sacred and the secular, the eternal and the everyday. The verses of these spiritual bards were sung at winter ceilidhs and at summer gatherings in the hill shielings or shelters. Their lifestyles, too, often echoed those of Columba and his fellow monks. Many regularly retreated to their own private places of prayer in the hills, like the late-eighteenth-century bard of Harris, Iain Gobha (Iain the Blacksmith), who wrote his verses after many hours of wrestling with the Almighty in his 'cell' amidst the rocks on which he had carved the simple words 'God is love'. It is significant that John Macinnes, author of the standard work on Highland evangelicalism, acknowledges Columba as 'the first of the Gaelic spiritual bards'.[16]

Traces of this deep and distinctive Columban spirituality are still clearly discernible in the Christian life and witness of the Presbyterian communities in the Western Isles. I suspect that it may well be in the utterly God-centred worship of the Gaelic-speaking congregations of the Church of Scotland, the Free Church and the Free Presbyterian Church in its stark simplicity and, to modern mainland taste, its rather severe and forbidding austerity that we get closer than anywhere else today to the spirit of worship on Columba's Iona. Instead of the buzz of idle chatter which precedes

most church services nowadays, there is an almost palpable still-
ness as worshippers take their places up to twenty minutes or so
before the start of the service simply to sit in silent prayer and contemplation without any visual or aural distraction, both musical
instruments and decoration or ornament of any kind being barred
from church buildings. There is an atmosphere of profound awe
and reverence before the mystery of God – undisturbed by the
cloying chords of keyboards or the relentlessly upbeat syncopation
of praise bands – that I think Columba would recognise and
appreciate. He would also feel at home with the sung parts of the
service, consisting as they do exclusively of unaccompanied
chanting of the Psalms. Gaelic metrical psalmody, with its
mournful and deeply moving cadences which seem to rise and fall
in time with the rhythm of the sea, bears certain clear resemblances
to the descriptions given of the chanting of psalms by the early
monks on Iona. It is also uncannily similar to the style of psalm
singing still practised in the Coptic church in Egypt and Ethiopia.
Could it be that preserved in the remote extremities of ancient
Christendom, in the eastern and far western Celtic fringes which
we know were once so closely linked, are the remnants of a once
universal Christian chant which may well have derived from the
synagogue and have been used by Jesus in his own worship?

If the Protestant churches of the northern part of the Outer
Hebrides may in some respects be the most faithful inheritors of
Columban Christianity, their Roman Catholic neighbours in the
southern isles have remained closer to its gentler and more mystical side. In such places as South Uist and Barra, the sense of
supernatural presences has survived and there is more inter-
weaving of the Christian and pre-Christian themes and influences.
It is significant that it was predominantly from the inhabitants of
these southern isles in the latter decades of the nineteenth century
that Alexander Carmichael collected the Gaelic prayers, blessings,

charms and incantations that went into his collection *Carmina Gadelica*. I have already expressed my own doubts about his claim that some of this material went back to Columba's time. They rather represent a much later strain of Christian spirituality, altogether less severe and ascetic, more affirmative of the natural world, and more congenial to the modern mind than the somewhat gloomy and doom-laden verses which have come down to us from sixth- and seventh-century Iona. The *Carmina* includes many charms and poems about Columba, including one about him conversing with a swan. His help is enlisted in herding sheep and milking cattle and his healing power invoked for indigestion and gum disease. One of the poems that Carmichael collected from fisher folk and crofters is about meeting Columba, Peter and Paul on the way to Rome. He also noted that in the Hebrides every Thursday was regarded as Columba's day and seen as a propitious time for embarking on any new task or venture:

> *Thursday of Columba benign,*
> *Day to send sheep on prosperity,*
> *Day to send cow on calf,*
> *Day to put the web in the warp.*
> *Day to put coracle on the brine,*
> *Day to place the staff to the flag,*
> *Day to bear, day to die,*
> *Day to hunt the heights.*
> *Day to put horses in harness,*
> *Day to send herds to pasture,*
> *Day to make prayer efficacious,*
> *Day of my beloved, the Thursday.*[17]

Iona continued to attract visitors in the centuries following the Reformation, many of them lured there by the appeal of Columba and his spiritual legacy. The Benedictine monks departed and worship ceased in the Abbey following the establishment of Protestantism in Scotland in 1560. The Abbey chancel was used for Protestant worship for another hundred years, after which there was no minister on the island until the building of the simple parish church in 1829. By the mid-eighteenth century the entire Abbey was in ruins, as were the other religious sites on the island. Visiting in 1772, the Welsh antiquarian Thomas Pennant had to bribe a local man to dig away a pile of cow dung on the floor of the nunnery to reveal Prioress Anna MacLean's grave slab. When James Boswell and Samuel Johnson came a year later, they were disappointed to find that virtually nothing remained of the early tombs in the Reilig Odhráin and that the Abbey floor was covered in mud and rubbish.

Successive Dukes of Argyll, whose family owned Iona from the 1690s, sought to conserve the island's religious fabric and heritage. In 1757 the third Duke enclosed the Abbey ruins with a wall in an effort to protect them and instructed his tenants to keep both the Abbey and the nunnery free from weeds and other 'nuisance'. John Walker wrote in 1764 of islanders using the Abbey for worship and there was a report in 1788 of local people dancing in the ruins. In 1797 the fifth Duke reprimanded his tenants for removing stones from the Abbey, although visitors were the chief culprits in vandalising its contents.

Columba's busy monastic hub, from which he regularly had to seek peace by going off to Hinba, became a place of calm, quiet retreat. Its romantic appeal was enhanced by its perceived isolation and ruined state, the empty buildings speaking more eloquently of the eternal mysteries than when they had been full of monks and nuns. William Wordsworth was somewhat nonplussed to be greeted on landing by a ragged child trying to sell him pebbles from the beach but penned a sonnet praising the spiritual atmosphere enveloping the island despite its rather desolate and dejected state. In the eyes of many visitors, the ruined aspect of the buildings added to the island's spiritual atmosphere. For Dr Johnson, who memorably remarked on Iona's power to make the piety of those who went there grow warmer, they were 'ruins of religious magnificence' serving as 'melancholy memorials to a lost age of faith'. An anonymous visitor in 1771 waxed even more lyrical: 'Nature has formed *Icolumbkill* for contemplation. In this solitary recess, sequestered from the follies and tumults which embroil the great world, the serious soul had leisure to think of heaven. Everything inspired sedate thought.'[18]

In the latter half of the nineteenth century antiquarianism, romanticism and heightened denominationalism combined to focus on Iona as the icon of that pure and primitive faith which was increasingly being labelled Celtic Christianity. Columba was claimed as a founding father by Episcopalians, by Presbyterians in the established Church of Scotland and by those in the more evangelical Free Church like Thomas M'Lauchlan whose book, *The Early Scottish Church* (1865), contrasted 'the ambitious, grasping spirit' of Augustine and his companions, 'covetous of place and power', with the humility of Columba and the missionaries of Iona and Lindisfarne, 'covetous of exalting Christ, but crucifying self'.[19] Roman Catholics insisted that they were the true heirs to the Iona saint but Protestant apologists remained unconvinced. William Ross, a Presbyterian minister, maintained in 1885 that it had been established 'beyond the power of reasonable contradiction, that no worship of the Virgin, or of saints, was sanctioned by Columba; that he gave no countenance to the doctrine of Purgatory; that Extreme Unction formed no part of his creed; and that, although some doubtful phrases do occur in reference to the Lord's Supper, communion at Iona was in both kinds'.[20]

The enthusiasm for Columba spread far beyond Iona. An English clergyman, Samuel Stone, rector of the City of London church of All Hallows' On the Wall and best remembered now for his hymn 'The Church's One Foundation', fell under the spell of Columba after visiting Iona while on holiday in Scotland in 1872 and began writing romantic poems about him and his legacy. In 1897 he gathered these together in a volume entitled *Lays of Iona* which called on the churches throughout the British Isles to return to their Celtic Columban roots. When a new outpost of the Church of Scotland was established at Pont Street in the fashionable West End of London in 1884, the decision was made to call it St Andrew's. However Donald MacLeod, its first minister, who was a Highlander, insisted it be St Columba's 'for the sacred isle of Iona possessed his heart'. A rose-shaped window in the church designed by Douglas Strachan showing Columba sitting at his writing desk and laying down his pen for the last time is one of many stained glass depictions of the saint which appeared in late Victorian and Edwardian times. Perhaps the most imposing is the great East window in Dunkeld Cathedral, installed in 1908, where Columba looks like a cross between Mr Gladstone and a Roman senator.

This renewed interest in Columba coincided with the period when Iona's owner was George Douglas, eighth Duke of Argyll, who had a deep personal interest in its religious history and spiritual significance. A remarkable polymath, who served as a Cabinet minister in every Whig and Liberal government between 1852 and 1881, he was a distinguished amateur philosopher, theologian, naturalist and geologist, as well as a talented poet and painter, and exemplified the intellectual, liberal, mystical Presbyterian faith of the Campbells. In 1870 he wrote a best-selling book which covered in detailed and scholarly fashion both Columba's life and times and also the later history of the Benedictine community on Iona. Four years later he initiated a major programme of structural repair work in the Abbey, the nunnery and St Oran's Chapel, all of which were in imminent danger of complete collapse. He personally supervised this rescue operation which took five years and involved substantial rebuilding as well as shoring up crumbling walls and removing several feet of rubble. Most of the carved stones which had been lying on the ground were moved to an upright position and placed against walls to afford them some protection.

In an important and influential lecture in 1895 James Cooper, a Church of Scotland minister and later Professor of Ecclesiastical History at Glasgow University, argued that the revival of Columban Christianity would lead to 'the healing of the divisions in Scottish Christianity'. He suggested that with Columba as a model, churches should draw more on those of high rank and noble birth and use 'the gifted sons of our nobles and chiefs' to provide both leaders and additional lay helpers to assist parish clergy. He also called for the erection of a network of replica high standing crosses in 'the numerous spots which are consecrated by saintly memories' as well as in churchyards and by the wayside. His most impassioned plea was for the restoration of the abbey buildings on Iona as a living embodiment of the whole Columban Christian tradition. He envisaged them becoming a theological college, ecumenical retreat house and school of Celtic art and music. Like the Duke of Argyll, he was attracted by the cross-denominational appeal of Columba and the potential that his legacy offered to unite Christians of different hues.[21]

In reality, Iona at this time symbolised nothing so much as the divided state of the church. Although the eighth Duke of Argyll allowed visiting clergy from both the Episcopalian and Roman Catholic churches to celebrate services within the walls of the ruined abbey, this was strongly opposed by many Presbyterians in the Church of Scotland and Free Church of Scotland who had the only churches on the island. A visiting Catholic priest lamented that 'no altar was there for the eucharistic sacrifice ... the poor people from the cradle to the grave were living without graces and dying without the blessing of true religion'.[22] Episcopalians fared little better. The island's Free Church minister had to be forcibly restrained when Bishop Ewing of the Scottish Episcopal Church ended an open-air service in the ruins with a Latin prayer. An islander later challenged the bishop to say how his ceremonies differed from those of the papists. Ewing's response 'If you had attended to my prayers you would have perceived a vast difference' was met with the retort 'Then why don't you pray in a language we can understand?'[23] When Ewing's successor, Alexander Chinnery-Haldane, sought in 1894 to establish a house on the island to be used as a place of Episcopalian prayer, study, and daily Eucharistic celebration, the parish minister raised a petition of 114 names opposing it. However, the Duke of Argyll was strongly of the opinion that those visiting Iona should be free to worship in their own way and, persuaded that what Chinnery Haldane had in mind was a place of prayer rather than proselytising, he granted permission for the building of what became known as Bishop's House. Situated at the end of the village, overlooking the Sound of Mull, it remains the Episcopal Church's base on the island today, providing comfortable accommodation and a chapel. A pointed arch niche in the east gable contains the only statue of Columba to be found on the island.

The celebrations held on Iona on 9 June 1897 to mark the 1300th anniversary of his death revealed just how far the major Scottish denominations were from finding unity in their common Columban inheritance. Gaelic and English services were conducted by the Church of Scotland in the Abbey, in which two hymns attributed to Columba, 'Christ is the World's Redeemer' and 'O God, Thou art the Father', were sung in translations provided for the occasion by Duncan MacGregor, a Church of Scotland minister who also gave an address describing him as 'the wisest of all the rulers of the Church of Scotland', enthusing about his devotion to Scripture, children and animals, and identifying his only weakness as a special affection for the Gael. MacGregor quoted Columba as saying, 'My nature is frail and I am yet carnal; for I cannot help loving the Scots more than any other nation.'[24] Clergy from the Scottish Episcopal Church held a separate commemoration on the same day in their new retreat house which was formally handed over into the care of the Society of St John the Evangelist, better known as the Cowley Fathers. Roman Catholics, whose request to come to the island on the day of the saint's death had been turned down, had to be content with a service a week later when 615 pilgrims arrived by steamer for a Pontifical High Mass. The *Oban Times* commented: 'A chance for the millennium was missed at Iona last week. Instead of three commemorations of St Columba, why not have had one combined celebration in the ancient fane of Iona?'[25]

Away from Iona, two prominent Scottish artists commemorated the 1300th anniversary of Columba's death in a more romantic and less partisan spirit. William McTaggart, paying his annual visit to his native Kintyre in June 1897, was moved to paint a picture of the saint arriving from Ireland at Gauldrons Bay near Machrihanish, which some historians have seen as another possible initial landing place on his journey from Ireland in 563. William Hole, a devout Episcopalian and earnest antiquarian who had been commissioned by the Scottish National Portrait Gallery in Edinburgh to paint a series of murals illustrating the most significant events in Scottish history, chose to devote the first tableau to Columba preaching to the Picts. He gave Columba and his followers proper Celtic tonsures, modelled his crozier on St Fillan's crozier in the collection of the National Museum of Scotland and based the Picts' weapons and jewellery on artefacts dating from the Bronze Age to the eleventh century. The result was a jumble of anachronisms – virtually none of the clothes or objects depicted in the mural actually dates from the sixth century – with a distinctly contemporary feel. Columba looks like a Victorian missionary preaching to a group of African villagers.

In the very last year of the nineteenth century, the Duke of Argyll relinquished ownership of all the ecclesiastical buildings on Iona and handed them over to a trust linked to the Church of Scotland. It was charged with re-roofing and restoring the abbey (or cathedral as it was called in the trust deeds) so that it could be used for public worship and with preserving and where appropriate restoring the other buildings. The trustees were also enjoined to allow all branches of the Christian Church to hold services within the restored abbey which was re-roofed and fitted out during the 1900s to make it suitable for worship once again.

Columba had a strong appeal to many of those involved in the more mystical and esoteric aspects of the Celtic Twilight movement in the early twentieth century. To them, he was a guardian of 'ancient wisdom' and friend of the Druids. For William Sharp, who wrote under the pseudonym of Fiona Macleod, he was the archetype of the spiritual Gael blessed with visionary and prophetic powers. In a meditation published in 1910 he wrote: 'I doubt if any other than a Gael can understand him aright. More than any Celt of whom history tells, he is the epitome of the Celt … He was the first of our race of whom is recorded the systematic use of the strange gift of spiritual foresight, "second-sight".'[26] Sharp also commented approvingly on the 'half-Pagan, half-Christian basis upon which the Columban church of Iona stood'.[27] Another prominent figure in the Scottish Celtic Revival movement, the artist John Duncan, painted 'St Columba Bidding Farewell to the White Horse' in 1925, drawing on an incident recounted in the last chapter of Adomnán's *Vita* and portraying the frail saint in his last hours on earth with the faithful horse which carried the milk round Iona nuzzling against him. In a book published in 1908 Victor Branford, a humanist, used Columba to illustrate the importance of pilgrimage in personal development, and in 1928 Eleanor Merry, a Theosophist, made him the central character in a play about spiritual forces older than Christianity. Rudolf Steiner, the Austrian philosopher and founder of anthroposophy, was greatly attracted to Columba and one of his followers who taught at the Waldorf School in Edinburgh wrote a play for young people based on the saint's life. Another play about him was written and performed by members of the Moral Re-Armament movement.

From a more orthodox Christian perspective, Lucy Menzies, a high church Episcopalian, wrote a glowing and widely read biography of Columba in 1920 which credited him, apparently single-handedly, with subduing the fierce passions of the Picts, securing the independence of the kingdom of the Scots, bringing civilisation to a lawless people and improving their methods of agriculture and their social relations. 'It is impossible for Scotland to exaggerate the debt she owes Columba,' she concluded, 'he founded her national unity, he brought about her inter-tribal peace and not only improved her whole mode of living, but set an ideal before her and brought to her the Bread of Life'.[28]

The 1930s saw the beginning of two major ventures inspired by Columba's example and legacy: the building of the Roman Catholic Cathedral in Oban and the restoration of the buildings around Iona Abbey. Both were long-term projects – work on the Cathedral began in 1932 and was not complete until 1959, while restoration of the abbey buildings started in 1935 and was finished in 1965. The architect for St Columba's Cathedral, Oban, was Giles Gilbert Scott, best known for the Anglican Cathedral in Liverpool and Battersea Power Station and for designing Britain's traditional red telephone boxes. The first cathedral anywhere in the world to be built entirely of granite, its restrained Gothic exterior provides a prominent landmark on the seafront for those entering Oban harbour by ferry. Inside the impression is of lofty simplicity and austerity. Appropriately, given its dedication, Columba is depicted at various points – twice on the reredos as well as in the dramatic painting by Nathaniel Westlake hanging over the entrance door which shows him calmly standing in a boat as he is banished down Loch Ness by pagan Druids. Woven into the main altar cloth in Gaelic is the verse from Psalm 34 which Adomnán described him copying just before his death: 'Those who seek the Lord shall not lack for anything.'

The rebuilding of the abbey buildings was carried out by work parties made up of skilled craftsmen and students from Scottish divinity faculties under the charismatic leadership of George Mac-Leod, a Church of Scotland minister who, like Columba, came of aristocratic stock, being the son of a baronet and Conservative MP. Educated at Winchester and Oxford, he retained a certain patrician manner and tone of voice throughout his life. Having regularly holidayed on Iona, he became increasingly convinced through the early 1930s that a project focused on rebuilding the living quarters of the Benedictine Abbey could foster the community spirit which he felt was desperately needed as a counter to the prevailing individualism of the age. In 1935 he put a paper to the Iona Cathedral Trustees proposing that skilled workers and candidates for the ministry should collaborate on restoring the buildings with a view to making them a Church of Scotland seminary which would inculcate in all ministers the values of brotherhood and communal life. His hope was that candidates for the Church of Scotland ministry would spend six months of each of their three years of training on Iona. The Trustees agreed to his proposal and in the summer of 1938 MacLeod took out his first party of students and craftsmen, several of them unemployed shipyard workers from his own parish in Govan, Glasgow. These summer work camps went on until 1965, by which time the cloisters, refectory, chapter house and dormitories had all been rebuilt.

Ringing in George MacLeod's ears was the prophecy supposedly uttered by Columba shortly before his death:

Iona of my heart, Iona of my love,
Instead of monks' voices there shall be lowing of cattle:
But ere the world comes to an end
Iona shall be as it was.

Shamelessly exploiting his aristocratic contacts, MacLeod persuaded his friends in high places to part with their money much as Columba had persuaded kings and princes to give land and endowments for his monastic foundations. In its early days the all-male Iona Community was run like a boys' public school with cold swims in the sea before breakfast and a strict regime in the dormitories at night. In his attempt to create an ecumenical Christian community relevant to the needs of the modern world, MacLeod was deeply influenced by his admiration for Columba and his understanding of the nature of the church that he had established on Iona. The newsletter that he started in October 1938 to record the progress of the project was named *The Coracle* after the type of leather-skinned boat which had brought the saint and his companions to the island. An incurable romantic with a rich imagination, MacLeod shamelessly made up stories about Columba to fit in with his own personal preoccupations and those who heard him talking about the saint were never quite sure whether he was referring to himself or his sixth-century predecessor. The two men were uncannily alike in many ways, sharing an aristocratic background, charismatic personality, visionary quality, deep prayerfulness, poetic flair and somewhat autocratic manner. As MacLeod himself might have remarked, 'If you call that a coincidence, I hope you have a very dull life.'

Despite his energy and charisma George MacLeod did not get quite what he wanted on Iona. When the Abbey buildings were finally finished and ready for occupation in 1965, the Iona Community, which he had set up in 1939 to foster brotherhood among his all-male team of ministers and manual workers, voted against his seminary plan and chose rather to make the Abbey a place for retreats, conferences and training. This is essentially what it has remained ever since. Although the Community, which now numbers around 270 members and over 1800 associate members of both sexes and many different denominations, has its headquarters in Glasgow, Iona remains its spiritual home. Hundreds of guests come every year to stay for a week in the Abbey or in the MacLeod Centre, built on the hill above it in 1988, to live and worship together and explore issues of justice, peace, spirituality and the integrity of creation. Hundreds more visitors to the islands attend services in the Abbey led by a resident group of staff and volunteers.

Iona Abbey remains a living Christian hub focused on building community, engaged spirituality and creative worship. Visitors sometimes express surprise and disappointment that there are no cowled monks walking quietly around its cloisters. Instead the buildings are filled by boisterous young volunteers from all over the world who come to work as cooks, cleaners, sacristans and maintenance workers to support the ministry of hospitality. Guests staying at the Abbey and the MacLeod Centre share the common life by helping in washing up, cutting vegetables and cleaning the toilets. Morning and evening worship in the Abbey Church flows naturally into and from the life and work of the day. The atmosphere of evangelical simplicity, practical muscular

Christianity and devotion tinged with open-minded mysticism is one that Columba himself would surely recognise and approve. The Abbey was the focus for the commemoration of the 1400th anniversary of Columba's death in June 1997, which was undertaken in a much more ecumenical spirit than a hundred years earlier, with Presbyterians, Roman Catholics and Episcopalians worshipping together. On 9 June the President of Ireland, Mary Robinson, flew in by helicopter to attend a service in the Abbey at which I had the honour of preaching. She had earlier opened an exhibition on Columba at Fionnphort on the Isle of Mull. This anniversary inspired other initiatives elsewhere commemorating the Iona saint, including the St Columba Trail through northern Ireland and western Scotland, developed by the *Colmcille* project which promotes Gaelic culture across Ireland and Scotland, and Columba 1400, a project centred on Skye devoted to leadership training, especially among young people.

It is Iona, and especially its abbey, which has remained the first port of call for those wishing to explore Columba's life and legacy. In 1999, an agreement was made to take the abbey and its associated buildings into the care of Historic Scotland, the public body responsible for caring for and conserving Scotland's built heritage, with the Iona Community leasing them for worship and residential purposes. In 2010 the Iona Cathedral Trust widened its ecumenical base, while retaining a strong Church of Scotland connection, and extended its remit 'to advance the education of the public in relation to the history, culture and heritage of Iona Cathedral and the Island of Iona'. In 2013, Historic Scotland, under the direction of Peter Yeoman, implemented a significant reinterpretation of the entire site, which can now be explored with excellent audio guides, and refurbished the museum in the old infirmary. Iona is one of the undoubted jewels in the crown of Historic Environment Scotland, as Historic Scotland became known in 2015.

Over 130,000 people visit Iona every year, many of them drawn by the romance and appeal of Columba. Some make their way to the bay at the south end where he supposedly landed and which bears his name, while others pause on their way up to the abbey to have a drink or a cup of tea at the St Columba Hotel. His story is told through displays in the museum and in the north transept of the Abbey where a pair of stone feet are all that remain of a probable medieval monument to him. He is also depicted in two stained glass windows in the Abbey, one in the north transept and the other high up in the east wall of the chancel.

Virtually nothing remains on Iona from Columba's lifetime. What visitors see today is the restored Benedictine Abbey established more than 600 years after his death. All that survives from his own monastery, which consisted of a number of simple huts made out of wood and wattle and daub, are the outlines in places of the boundary *vallum* or ditch and the presumed site of his own austere cell on Tòrr an Aba, the mound in front of the Abbey. Radio carbon dating undertaken in 2017 on burned hazel stakes found on this site give a date range of between 540 and 640, suggesting that it is likely that it was occupied during his time on the island and so could, indeed, have been his dwelling place and/or writing hut. The high standing crosses and dramatic Street of the Dead post-date Columba's life by at least 150 years, as does the restored shrine chapel to the left of the entrance to the Abbey where his remains lay before being removed from the island to prevent their seizure by Viking raiders. These striking features of Iona's spiritual landscape testify to the power of a dead saint rather than to his faith or activities when alive. It is not entirely clear where his remains now lie but they are probably divided between Kells and Dunkeld.

It is in the work of the Iona Community, carried out on the mainland as much as in the Abbey and the MacLeod Centre on

Iona and at Camas Tuath, based around an old fishing hut on the Ross of Mull used for youth groups, that the legacy of Columba perhaps lives on most faithfully and practically in prayer and penitence, political engagement, and commitment to justice, reconciliation and peace. The Community's Wild Goose Resource Group, based in Glasgow, has had a major impact on the worship of churches across the world, through encouraging much more use of the Psalms, not least the darker and less upbeat ones, as expressed in the title of one of its many songbooks, *Psalms of Patience, Protest and Praise.* It has also been responsible for many new prayers and songs which exhibit the poetic quality of Columban spirituality while dealing with contemporary concerns. It seems appropriate to end this chapter with a song written by two of its members, John Bell and the late Graham Maule, which both celebrates the achievements of Columba and his contemporaries and calls us to follow them.

From Erin's shores Columba came
To preach and teach and heal,
And found a church which showed the world
How God on earth was real.

In greening grass and reckless wave,
In cloud and ripening corn,
The Celtic Christians traced the course
Of grace through nature borne.

In hosting strangers, healing pain,
In tireless work for peace,
They served the servant Christ their Lord
And found their faith increase.

In simple prayer and alien land,
As summoned by the Son,
They celebrated how God's call
Made work and worship one.

God grant that what Columba sowed
May harvest yet more seed,
As we engage both flesh and faith
To marry word and deed.

Notes

1   *Life of Columba*, p.6
2   *Bede's Ecclesiastical History of England*, p.143
3   Alfred Smyth, *Warlords and Holy Men*, p.7
4   Ian Muirhead, 'The beginnings' in *Studies in the History of Worship in Scotland* (eds. Duncan Forrester and Douglas Murray) (T & T Clark,Edinburgh, 1996), p.5
5   *Bede's Ecclesiastical History of England*, p.142
6   Smyth, *Warlords and Holy Men*, p.33
7   *Bede's Ecclesiastical History of England*, p.193
8   *Ibid.*, pp.197-200
9   Shirley Toulson, *The Celtic Alternative* (Century Hutchison, London, 1987), pp.10-11
10   Ian Cowan, 'The Post-Columban church' in *Records of the Scottish Church History Society*, No.18 (1974), p.259
11   Sally Foster, *Picts, Gaels and Scots*, p.113
12   On the music of the Inchcolm Antiphoner, see John Purser, *Scotland's Music* (Mainstream Publishing, Edinburgh, 1992), pp.39-45. The Lauds for the Feast of Columba are recorded by Cappella Nova on CD on the Gaudeamus label.
13   Ursula Hall, *St Andrew and Scotland* (St Andrews University Library, St Andrews, 1994)

14   Donald Meek, *The Scottish Highlands* (Gospel and Culture Pamphlet 11, World Council of Churches, Geneva, 1996), pp.36-7

15   There is an excellent article on 'The Men' by Donald Meek in the *Dictionary of Scottish Church History and Theology* (T & T Clark, Edinburgh, 1993), pp.558-59

16   John Macinnes, *The Evangelical Movement in the Highlands of Scotland 1688 to 1800* (Aberdeen University Press, Aberdeen, 1951), p.265

17   Alexander Carmichael, *Carmina Gadelica* (Floris Books, Edinburgh, 1992), p.80

18   Richard Sharpe, 'Iona in 1771', *Innes Review*, Vol.63, No.2 (Autumn 2012), p.197

19   Ian Bradley, *Celtic Christianity: Making Myths and Chasing Dreams* (Edinburgh University Press, Edinburgh, 1999), p.131

20   William Ross, *Aberdour and Inchcolme* (David Douglas, Edinburgh, 1855), p.58

21   *The Divine Life of the Church* (Scottish Church Society Conference, 2nd series, Edinburgh, 1895), Vol.II, pp.15-44

22   Bradley, *Celtic Christianity*, p.147

23   Bradley, *Celtic Christianity*, p.148

24   Duncan MacGregor, *St Columba: A Record and a Tribute* (J. Gardner Hitt, Edinburgh, 1897), p.65

25   D.P. Thompson, *Iona to Ardnamurchan* (Blackwood, Edinburgh, 1956), p.3

26   Fiona Macleod, 'Iona' in *The Works of Fiona Macleod*, Vol.IV (Heinemann, London, 1910), pp.130 & 134

27   *Ibid.*, p.241

28   Lucy Menzies, *Saint Columba of Iona* (J.M. Dent, London, 1920), p.194

Epilogue

Our journey –
politics, penitence and pilgrimage

Does Columba have anything to say to us today, 1500 years after his birth? Can he help us and guide us along our own faith journeys?

I am very conscious that it is all too easy to co-opt him in support of our own preferred theologies, denominational allegiances and ways of doing things. In the words of Donald Meek: 'Columba is adaptable. He has shown a capacity to be relevant to the needs of many phases of history … Since at least the first century of his death, Columba has been the flexible friend of a wide variety of seekers and, of course, finders who have not hesitated to use his good offices for their own earthly purposes.'[1] He has, as we have seen, been enlisted and claimed over the years by Roman Catholics, Episcopalians, Presbyterians of various hues, humanists, anthroposophists and neo-pagan Celtic revivalists. He has proved to be a singularly adaptable and all-purpose saint, in death if not in life.

What comes over most clearly in the various poems and lives written about him in the decades immediately following his death is Columba's austerity and self-denial. It is there in Beccán mac Luigdech's description of him crucifying his body on the grey waves, in Adomnán's reference to his engagement day and night 'in the unwearied exercise of fasting and watching' and in the *Irish Life*'s stark portrayal of his ribs showing through his cloak as he lay on the shore chanting all 150 psalms before daybreak. He comes across as a somewhat stern and severe figure, certainly in the way that he treated himself. Every Wednesday morning worshippers in Iona Abbey say together a prayer which enumerates Columba's God-given gifts as 'courage, faith and cheerfulness'. Courage and faith he did, indeed, have in plenty but there is precious little evidence of him ever being cheerful. He is certainly not an exemplar of the rather appealing and relatively undemanding creed that now passes as Celtic Christianity. To quote

Donald Meek again, 'His flesh-subduing austerity – not a prominent theme in modern "Celtic Christianity" stands in sharp contrast to the narcissism of contemporary political philosophy.'[2]

This all seems rather forbidding, and very different from the reassuring, comforting and idealised image of the saint at his writing desk which first drew me to him and is reproduced on the cover of this book. But there was a gentler side to Columba, especially in his dealings with others. It is expressed in the last words that he addressed to his brethren on Iona shortly before he died and which have been adapted into a moving modern exhortation:

> *See that you be at peace among yourselves, my children,*
> *and love one another.*
> *Follow the example of good men of old,*
> *and God will comfort you and help you*
> *both in this world and in the world which is to come.*

The promotion of peace among ourselves is surely one of Columba's most important messages for us today in our age of increasingly ill-tempered anger and intolerance fuelled by social media. So are those other themes beginning with 'p' that I identified in Chapter 4 as characterising the Columban church: prayerfulness, expressing faith in poetic terms, making more use of the Psalms in devotion and worship and cultivating a disposition to praise. Invoking God's protective power through modern versions of the breastplate (*lorica*) and encircling (*caim*) prayers can be helpful to the many who today suffer mental illness and feel anxious, threatened and bullied or abused. A ministry of steady pastoral presence, such as that practised by Columba on Iona, is just as much needed now as it was in the sixth century. So, too, is a sense of the essentially provisional nature of all structures and human institutions, including the church, and a resolve to create more fluid and less fixed Christian communities. I have written much more fully about these particular Columban characteristics in my book *Following the Celtic Way* (Darton, Longman and Todd, 2018).

Three features perhaps stand out particularly in Columba's life, faith and ministry – the three 'p's of politics, penitence and pilgrimage that I highlighted in Chapter 1 of this book. He was undoubtedly in some respects a politician, certainly a political animal. He was involved in the dynastic and tribal disputes of his Uí Néill relatives, attended conventions in Ireland, negotiated with the rulers of the kingdoms that would eventually make up Scotland and ran his own monastic *familia* much as a king would rule his *túath*. As we have seen, he acted as a kingmaker, choosing and possibly also ordaining the kings of Dál Riata and putting the church's support behind the relatively new institution of monarchy which he believed made for the rule of justice, mercy and stability in contrast to the power struggle between warlords and tribal chiefs which had hitherto prevailed.

Christians today are surely called to political awareness and activism. There are glaring injustices and inequalities in our world, many of them getting worse rather than better; there are flagrant abuses of human rights; and there is the threat to our planet and our own survival as a species posed by global warming, loss of species and biodiversity, and pollution of the environment. Political engagement and lobbying, of the kind that the Iona Community has been engaged in throughout its history on issues related to peace, justice and the integrity of creation, stand very much in the Columban tradition.

For Columba, political involvement went alongside a deep sense of penitence, repentance and contrition. His sense of his own vulnerability and unworthiness is evident in his description of himself in *Adiutor Laborantium* as 'a little man trembling and most wretched, rowing through the infinite storm of this age' and in these lines from the poem attributed to him and quoted at the end of Chapter 3 when, after invoking the hill on Iona known as Cul ri Erin (Back turned to Ireland), he prays

> *That contrition might come upon my heart*
> *Upon looking at her;*
> *That I might bewail my evils all,*
> *Though it were difficult to compute them.*

There is a similar note of profound humility and unworthiness in another much-used prayer attributed to Columba which I have not yet quoted in this book:

> *Almighty God,*
> *Father, Son, and Holy Spirit*
> *to me the least of saints,*
> *to me allow that I may keep*
> *even the smallest door,*
> *the farthest, darkest, coldest door,*
> *the door that is least used,*
> *the stiffest door.*
> *If only it be in your house, O God,*
> *that I can see your glory even afar,*
> *and hear your voice,*
> *and know that I am with you, O God.*

Without descending into masochistic self-chastisement or Uriah-Heep-style grovelling, an attitude of humility and penitence is an important and perhaps a somewhat neglected part of the Christian condition and calling. We have much to be penitent about at both an individual and a corporate level in respect of our spiritual pride, our hypocrisy, our judgmentalism and the sickening abuse which has been uncovered in our churches over recent years. We need not wallow in our sinfulness, and we certainly need constantly to forgive ourselves as well as to forgive others, but we also need something of Columba's very evident and genuine sense of penitence, contrition and humility.

More positively, Columba calls us to follow him as pilgrims. Growing interest in pilgrimage has been one of the most striking aspects of the spiritual landscape of Europe over recent decades. I have written about it in my book *Pilgrimage: A Spiritual and Cultural Journey* (2009). Old pilgrim routes have been revived and a plethora of new pilgrim ways established across the British Isles and Continental Europe – one of them, the Fife Pilgrim Way, is the subject of another of my recent books, published in 2019. On the face of it, this modern kind of pilgrimage is very different indeed from the *peregrinatio* practised by the Irish monks. It is about travelling to holy places, often in the comfort of cars, trains or luxury coaches, and getting a spiritual buzz from visiting them, rather than about experiencing the sense of exile that animated Columba.

Yet in several respects the contemporary enthusiasm for pilgrimage does echo the Celtic theme of *peregrinatio*. It accords with the way that increasing numbers of people see their faith. Surveys suggest that far more Christians now than in previous generations describe their faith as an ongoing journey rather than as a sudden decisive conversion experience. The road to Emmaus, along which the resurrected Jesus travelled with two of his disciples for many miles before they recognised him, seems to resonate with more believers nowadays than the road to Damascus on which Paul underwent a sudden blinding conversion. Pilgrimage has much to offer in an age such as ours where there is so much anxiety, yearning and seeking and where so many feel disconnected from roots and traditions.

The actual physical pilgrimages which are being made by more and more Christians also resonate with key themes in Columban Christianity. They often manifest an embodied physical spirituality and tie in with concern about the environment and also with promoting fitness and combating obesity. Modern pilgrims may not subject themselves to the severe and rigorous austerity that seems to have characterised Columba's life but they are similarly modelling an approach to faith which is physical as well as intellectual and active as well as passive. There is a growing interest in walking rather than just talking the faith. As fewer people are prepared to sit passively in churches on a Sunday morning being preached at, more are happy to go on prayer walks, use labyrinths and undertake pilgrimages.

There is also much enthusiasm for recovering the notion, prevalent in the early church, of Christians as followers of the Way. This has many different dimensions. It may mean leading more intentional lives, perhaps in dispersed communities following a prescribed rule of life. It may mean sitting more loosely to structures and hierarchies, being more inclusive, more open to new ideas and more prepared to take risks. Many Christians now involve themselves in protest vigils, walks, marches and demonstrations for peace and justice, or in sponsored swims, walks and cycle rides. Perhaps these are the new pilgrimages for our age, often undertaken with those of other faiths and those of no faith. For Christians, the Way will always involve following the one who had nowhere to lay his head and carried out his peripatetic ministry, teaching, preaching and healing as he journeyed along.

Particular emphases that we find within Columba's life, as it has been recounted by his early eulogists and biographers, can help us in our own pilgrim journeys. There is the balance that he struck between *peregrinatio* and presence. On the face of it, these seem conflicting themes, the one emphasising movement, restless journeying and perpetual wandering, and the other stability, steady availability and being there for others. He combined them in an unforced rhythm of faith and life, just as he combined periods of intense involvement in political affairs and monastic administration with lengthy retreats to Hinba to be alone with God.

Following Columba the pilgrim means venturing beyond our comfort zone, being prepared to go to places and experience situations which may make us uneasy, taking the risk of wasting time, getting lost and letting go. It means casting off from the familiar and the comfortable, just as he did when he left his beloved Ireland in 563, seeing our life and our faith as an ongoing journey, being ever open to new possibilities, while always trusting in God and in God's protective power. These themes are brought together in a poem attributed to Columba and translated from the original Irish by an unknown hand around 1911. I end this book with it because I feel that it encapsulates his life, faith and trust as both pilgrim and penitent.

Alone with none but thee, my God,
I journey on my way:
what need I fear when thou art near,
O King of night and day?
More safe am I within thy hand
than if a host should round me stand.

My destined time is known to thee,
and death will keep his hour;
did warriors strong around me throng,
they could not stay his power:
no walls of stone can man defend
when thou thy messenger dost send.

My life I yield to thy decree,
and bow to thy control
in peaceful calm, for from thine arm
no power can wrest my soul:
could earthly omens e'er appal
a man that heeds the heavenly call?

The child of God can fear no ill,
his chosen dread no foe;
we leave our fate with thee, and wait
thy bidding when to go:
'tis not from chance our comfort springs,
thou art our trust, O King of kings.

Notes

1   *Spes Scotorum: Hope of the Scots*, edited by Dauvit Brown and Thomas
    Owen Clancy (T & T Clark, Edinburgh, 1999), pp.268, 269.
2   *Ibid.*, p.269

Suggestions for further reading

The two most recent biographies of Columba are Tim Clarkson's *Columba* (John Donald, Edinburgh, 2012) and Brian Lacey's *Saint Columba: His Life and Legacy* (Columba Press, Dublin, 2013). Both are excellent, the former focusing largely on his years in Scotland and the latter having more about his time and legacy in Ireland. Ian Finlay's *Columba* (Victor Gollancz, 1979) is also still worth reading. The most recent and comprehensive edition of Adomnán's *Life of Columba* is that edited by Richard Sharpe (Penguin Books, London, 1995) which has a valuable introduction and helpful notes. The full text of the medieval *Irish Life* can be found in Máire Herbert's scholarly and informative study of the history and hagiography of the monastic *familia* of Columba, *Iona, Kells and Derry* (Four Courts Press, Dublin, 1996).

Judith McClure and Roger Collins have edited a clear and accessible edition of Bede's *The Ecclesiastical History of the English People* (Oxford University Press, Oxford, 1999). The earliest poems from Iona, including those most likely to have been written by Columba, have been brought together and superbly translated with accompanying commentaries by Thomas Owen Clancy and Gilbert Márkus in *IONA: The Earliest Poetry of a Celtic Monastery* (Edinburgh University Press, Edinburgh, 1995).

Columba's legacy is the subject of a fine collection of essays edited by Dauvit Brown and Thomas Owen Clancy entitled *Spes Scotorum: Hope of Scots. Saint Columba, Iona and Scotland* (T & T Clark, Edinburgh, 1999). The history of Iona is well covered in Rosalind Marshall's *Columba's Iona: A New History* (Sandstone Press, Dingwall, 2013) which was commissioned by the Iona Cathedral Trust. There is also much to be enjoyed in a collection of verse and prose edited by Robert Crawford, *The Book of Iona: An Anthology* (Polygon, Edinburgh, 2016).

Columba's footprint in Argyll is discussed and illustrated at more length in my *Argyll: The Making of a Spiritual Landscape* (St Andrew Press, Edinburgh, 2015). There is also much about the saint in what I am pretty sure will be my last word on the subject of Celtic Christianity, *Following the Celtic Way* (Darton, Longman and Todd, 2018).

Wild Goose Publications, the publishing house of the Iona Community established in the Celtic Christian tradition of Saint Columba, produces books, e-books, CDs and digital downloads on:

- holistic spirituality
- social justice
- political and peace issues
- healing
- innovative approaches to worship
- song in worship, including the work of the Wild Goose Resource Group
- material for meditation and reflection

For more information:

Wild Goose Publications
The Iona Community
Suite 9, Fairfield, 1048 Govan Road
Glasgow G51 4XS, Scotland

Tel. +44 (0)141 429 7281
e-mail: admin@ionabooks.com

or visit our website at
www.ionabooks.com
for details of all our products and online sales